my 1,000 americans

my 1,000 americans

A Year-Long Odyssey Through the Personals

ROCHELLE MORTON

 THREE RIVERS PRESS
NEW YORK

Individuals' names and certain characteristics have been changed to protect their identities.

Copyright © 2001 by Rochelle Morton
Illustrations © 2001 by Pamela Hobbs, www.pamarama.com

Published by Three Rivers Press, New York, New York.
Member of the Crown Publishing Group.

Random House, Inc. New York, Toronto, London, Sydney, Auckland
www.randomhouse.com

THREE RIVERS PRESS is a registered trademark and the Three Rivers Press colophon is a trademark of Random House, Inc.

Printed in the United States of America

DESIGN BY JANE TREUHAFT

Library of Congress Cataloging-in-Publication Data

Morton, Rochelle.
  My 1,000 Americans: a year-long odyssey through the personals /
  by Rochelle Morton.
  1. Dating (Social customs)   2. Personals.   3. Man-woman
  relationships.   I. Title: My one thousand Americans.   II. Title: My
  thousand Americans.   III. Title.

HQ801 .M785 2001
646.7'7—dc21   2001023463

ISBN 0-609-80500-2

10 9 8 7 6 5 4 3 2 1

First Edition

for

my son

who will always be the best date
a girl could ever have

contents

introduction

Take a look at that ad.

Not many words, and hardly provocative. Yet it generated almost two thousand replies from men in five different states! I was of course pleased by the number of responses my demure ad generated, but I wasn't entirely surprised, as I wasn't a complete novice to the personal ads. You see, a year ago I had placed a similar ad in a newspaper in London, England (that's where I'm from and, yes, I do know the Queen). When I got a thunderous response, I decided to date as many of my respondents as I humanly could, nearly seven hundred in the end, and wrote up the experience in a book entitled *Eat Your Lonely Heart Out*.

At that time I was happily ensconced in a relationship but surrounded by three female friends bemoaning the fact that they didn't have a man in their lives. After one particularly ear-bending evening with one of the three, I picked up the local paper and flung it at her, saying, "Look at all the guys in there. Call some of them; they can't all be jerks." At first she resisted, feeling it looked a bit desperate, but after a glass or two of medium-priced wine she agreed to give it a go. Together we created our own ad . . . for her. No sooner was the ad published than we found messages from seventy men on her voicemail. (I had actually begun to wonder how sad we would be if we had heard the "You have no messages" voice.) I could hardly wait for my friend to get out there and start meeting all those guys.

You can imagine my disappointment when my dear friend backed out on me after I had set the wheel in motion, but back out she did—seemingly onto the lap of a fellow she happened to meet in a local coffee bar; so all was not entirely lost. But having listened to all the replies, I became fascinated with the whole personals phenomenon, and I found myself calling in obsessively to check for new messages. (Can you imagine how good my boyfriend felt about that?) It was incredible to me that so many men had found the ad appealing enough to leave a message, and the diversity of the respondents was pretty surprising too. Who knew there were so many men reading the personal ads? Certainly not me! Anyway, I really felt there was a story there. With the bemused approval of my steady, I determined to meet these men myself and see what made them answer our ad, and that's just what I did—all seven hundred of them. We met at restaurants, cafés, and eateries of all descriptions, inspiring the title of my book.

What a difference a year makes. When I undertook my first foray into the world of the personals, it was strictly for research. I did have a man in my life, and we were on our way to the altar. Alas, we never did get there; seems he met another lass along the way. So when I was asked to take it upon myself to try the same research across the pond, I was only too willing. Having long been a fan of the United States and its menfolk (I like the females too, but not like that, thank you), it seemed the ideal way to go to work and maybe meet the man of my dreams along the way. I was eager to find out what types of American men would respond to my ad and why, and though from past experience I knew there would be a fair share of the good, the bad, and the ugly, I was filled with pleasurable anticipation.

*　*　*

I lost no time in placing my first ad, choosing a Florida newspaper purely because I had friends there—and I figured that should this turn out to be not such a great idea, I could at least chill out on the beach.

Sadly, my tan would have to wait. No sooner had the ad made its first appearance than my voicemail box was crammed with messages from guys claiming to be bankers, Wall Street highflyers, property developers and car salesmen, doctors, and lawyers . . . lots of lawyers. (By the way, have you noticed that the Sunshine State is shaped like a gun?) Ads placed in Atlanta, Chicago, and New York City yielded equally overwhelming results. (Note to any of my British countrymen and -women living in the U.S.: Keep the accent, love, it still works!)

I realized I was going to have to devise a system for meeting all these guys. After all, dating only the men who sounded appealing wouldn't exactly give me the kind of random sampling I was after, and although it probably would have been a great deal more fun for me to live through, it wouldn't be as much fun for you, dear reader, to experience vicariously. So I adopted the "delete, delete, meet" rule, erasing two out of every three calls, and contacting all those who were left, regardless of what they sounded like. Well, almost, anyway! If he was entertaining himself in a very personal way, or said anything even vaguely menacing, I rang off and moved on.

Yet even after such ruthless winnowing, I was still left with over a thousand potential dates. With grim determination I got out my day planner and started making engagements for breakfast, lunch, dinner, and drinks, sometimes all four in a single day. While I will agree that it was certainly a lot more fun than, say, "going down the mines," it was hard going at times.

Right around now you may be wondering exactly what kind of monster I am, leading on not one or two but a full thousand men with nothing on their minds but making a meaningful connection with someone they could share their lives with. Believe me, if that were the case I *would* be feeling a bit ashamed of myself. Fortunately for my conscience (and unfortunately for the women looking for the same), such guys are the minority, as you will see. As for the handful that were there with the best of intentions, be assured that I did them no harm. I am a nice person to date. I always dress nicely, arrive on time, and pay my share of the tab, and I don't have any dead animals about my person (all will become clear later, I promise). Never once did I suggest wrapping my companion in cling film, and I listened to their sexual peccadillos and other peculiar pastimes and preferences with as much equanimity as possible. What more can you expect from a perfect stranger?

So what did I learn? That men are men the whole world round, and that the similarities between the American men I met and those I met in England were more striking than the differences. The guy who describes himself as a Richard Gere lookalike in America is no more likely to resemble him than the Brit who says he's a dead ringer for Daniel Day-Lewis. Married men are no more faithful on one side of the pond than the other, and there are plenty of men in both places whose expectations, shall we say, outstrip reality. Why a three-hundred-pound, middle-aged, unemployed computer salesman should consider himself a magnet for slender young blondes is a mystery to me.

I discovered that although in a lot of publications these personal ads are called "lonely hearts," in truth in many cases it's not the hearts that are in need of a little TLC. (Then again, there aren't a lot of papers that will run lonely penis ads.) I became counselor and therapist to a couple of guys who had reached rock bottom. Of course there were the dates that reached for *my* bottom, but we'll get to that in a bit. Seemingly intelligent men asked me questions about British royalty and believed whatever I told them, and dozens of married men shared intimate personal details about their families and wives without knowing anything at all about me. For all they knew, I could have been writing a book!

Some of the other men I met had very bizarre sexual tastes, which they found they could discuss with me over pretzels or cocktails. I began to realize that from their point of view it was a numbers game; if you tell enough women that you'd like to pee over them, there's a good chance one of them might have a potty problem too. Oh, they may encounter a few slaps along the way, but if you don't ask, you don't get.

By no means was every date a disaster. There are some wonderful men out there; you just have to find them. True, you'll probably have to kiss a lot of frogs (or at least share a pizza with them) before you do, but keep trying. (Read the chapter on nice guys if you need further encouragement.) For those of you who think it's not very safe to meet men in such numbers, and with such a liberal screening policy, I thank you for your concern, but I was always careful. While I certainly did arrange to get together with men who hinted at "special interests" or seemed a brick short of a load, never did I meet with anyone who threatened me or suggested dangerous sexual encounters on the phone, and when I found myself in the presence of such a guy, I terminated the date, pronto. If you're ready to dip your toe into the personals dating pool, heed these general rules of thumb . . . please.

1. Never give out any personal information, including your home or cell phone number.
2. If he starts speaking about his body parts or yours, hang up.
3. Never . . . ever . . . meet at his home or yours.
4. Don't wear revealing or sexy clothes on your first (or second) date.

5. Never leave your drink unattended. If you must, then order a fresh one when you return.

6. Always meet at a restaurant or a well-populated public space. Avoid the movies or theaters, which put you too close to one another and don't allow the opportunity to get acquainted.

7. Always offer to pay your share of the expenses. That way there are no obligations.

8. Leave the venue on your own: Drive or take a cab.

Some men can be dazzlingly charming on the phone, but no matter how good a game they talk, recognize that there is no substitute for taking your time in getting to know someone. If you have an immediate personal connection that seems too good to be true, it may well be; and in any event, time and deeper acquaintance will only strengthen your connection. If he gets mad because you won't spill the beans on your home phone number and address, let him go. If he says, "Don't you trust me?" say, "No, I don't. I don't know you." Some of the guys I met told me that they had indeed gone to a woman's home on a first meeting, and that women had met them at their homes too. *Don't.*

So this is one Englishwoman's foray into the personal ad world in the United States—and I've got to tell you, I've never had so much fun. And remember, men are like buses: there's always another one 'round the corner.

the european connection

Since I have been in the States, I've noticed that whenever a cosmetics company or salon wants to confer instant cachet on their product, they describe it as "European" or "Europe's favorite," as in European facial, and "Now Europe's favorite mascara is available here." I have even seen an advertisement for Europe's favorite ironing board. (Hello? It would only be my favorite if it would do all the ironing itself.) A recent ad raved about "shopping in a European atmosphere." What would that mean to me? A cold, rainy place that charges six bucks a gallon for gas? The irony is that in England they use the reverse marketing strategy, touting the U.S.A. as the land of miracle creams and potions.

As we all know, neither location has magical properties, but somehow we still fall for the romance of the foreign, the exotic, and the unusual. It's no different in the personals. Because I identified myself as English and recorded my voicemail message in my homegrown British accent, I was inundated with hundreds of replies from men convinced that I was the hottest import since the Beatles. They felt I was exotic, classy, and somehow special, and they wanted to meet me just because I was European! (Not a bad thing.) One generous soul said, "You speak this language of ours so well." (Excuse me? Language of yours?) Aside from the guys who "loved my accent," others felt we had a "connection" due to their European heritage, be it real or imaginary. And of course there were the men who were so sophisticated and well traveled that only a European woman could appreciate their charms.

I lost count of the number of times I was asked about The Queen, Princess Diana (although most Americans still call her Lady Diana), Benny Hill, Monty Python, and a tall guy named John who their mother knew. Now, granted my sampling was not entirely random, but few of these Anglophiles were themselves terribly worldly. Few owned a passport, and a great many had never left their own state. Some, in fact, had never left their trailer park. I was stunned by how provincial some of these guys were. With all the terrible things happening in the world, the average American news station leads its broadcast with a headline along the lines of "Montgomery County introduces mandatory school uniforms . . . details at eleven." A man from Oregon asked me what apartheid was. Another had no idea who King Hussein was, or for that matter where Jordan was (and no, I don't mean Michael). One man I met in Florida astutely noted that I didn't take too much ice in my soda, which, according to him, was a "European thing." Especially perplexing was a man who, when I mentioned Poland, looked up at the ceiling as if in deep thought, then asked seriously, "Poland . . . is that Holland?" I assured him that it most certainly was—it was easier that way!

Nor did the fellows I met know much more about their alleged "homelands." What is it with Americans who profess "I'm Italian" or "I'm German"? Most of them can't say a single word in their "native" tongue, and if you ask what town their forebears were from, they haven't a clue. I have since been told that because the country is such a hotchpotch of different cultures, Americans choose an identity they like and stick with it. I think that's kind of fun—that way you can be from almost anywhere you want.

All these men (and many others as well) claimed that they chose my ad primarily because of the European connection, fragile as it may have seemed to me. So here go my attempts at international diplomacy. . . .

Paul, 32
Electrical Products Salesman
SINGLE

Paul sounded a bit hung up on appearances, though I didn't know *how* much until we met. His message said he was a very nice looking man, and he was also at pains to tell me that he had lots of hair that wasn't receding at all. I returned his call at his place of work, and we agreed to meet for lunch on his day off. Just before we hung up, he said, "What shall I wear for you?"

"Oh, just something casual," I replied. "It's only lunch." I detected that he seemed a little disappointed at that answer, but what the hell.

I arrived a few minutes late, but I wished I hadn't come at all when I spotted Paul in a corner of the restaurant. There he sat, dressed as a king! I kid you not: The man was in full monarch's regalia, with some kind of robe around his shoulders and a crown on his head. As I approached him, he stood up, tipped his crown, and said, "See, I told you I have lots of hair." Funny, but how much hair he had wasn't paramount in my mind right then. The waiter who had shown me to the table had tears in his eyes from laughing, but Paul seemed oblivious to this. "You are dressed like Lady Diana and Fergie," he announced approvingly, gesturing to my long, plain black skirt. In fact the only reason for this attire was that it had been quite chilly when I had set out, but to Paul the long skirt was "fit for a princess!"

I soon learned that Paul dressed as a king to "alleviate the boredom of selling cheap electrical goods to cheap people." Apparently the company he worked for didn't treat him too well, so on his day off, he liked to be king. Paul was not delusional, though. He told me over a regal repast of pasta and garlic bread that he spent his free time inspecting his apartment building for faults. He would then report them to the manager and see how long it took for them to be repaired or replaced. In his five years there he had single-handedly managed to get three managers fired, a fact of which he was extremely proud. He was indeed a prince among men.

When I asked why he had answered my ad, his answer was simple: "You're English, so you know about royalty. Americans just don't." I nodded solemnly as if in agreement, noting with relief that our check had arrived. I thanked him for meeting me and offered to pay my share. To my surprise he asked that I pay his share too, as monarchs don't carry cash. The meal was under twenty dollars so I paid up, thinking he'd gone to an awful lot of trouble for a $7.95 bowl of spaghetti. I got off lightly, really—we could have rendezvoused at a five-star restaurant. And it could have been worse—he could have been Henry VIII. Then who knows *what* trouble his building manager and I would have been in! ❤

Michael, 38
Realtor
SINGLE

Michael identified himself as Slavic when we arranged our date. I didn't press for more information, as he was in a hurry, but he said he'd just had to call when he saw my ad because we shared a European background. When we met, he spoke at length of how bad he felt for the people of Kosovo, and though I agreed it was a terrible thing, he felt I couldn't truly understand his pain. After all, he said, "I am Slavic, remember? My mother was from somewhere or other like that." I wondered how that keen sense of geography served him when selling a house. "Oh, it's a beautiful property, great location somewhere or other."

Michael was wearing the brightest multicolored shirt I had ever seen in my life, and I have seen a lot of shirts in my time. This one was dazzling, to say the least. I tactfully didn't comment on it, though when he asked me what I thought about it, I said it was very nice. (Well, you have to tell a little lie occasionally, to keep the peace!)

He was very hyper and talked nonstop about himself. More than anything, he wanted to be a millionaire and retire by the time he was fifty. Well, there is nothing wrong with ambition, but after an hour and a half of the life and times of Michael, during which he spoke at length about his controlling mother who dressed him only in the color fawn until he was eleven (hence the loud shirt, I guess), I'd had enough. I thanked him for meeting me and he did likewise. Then he offered me a little advice. Apparently I was too quiet; the next time I went on a date, he confided, I needed to speak more. No problem; next time I go on a date, it won't be with you, Michael, so maybe I'll get a word in edgewise. ❤

Allen, 39
Insurance Agent
SINGLE

Allen's European connection was a Belgian brother-in-law called Dettol. In England, Dettol is a well-known brand of disinfectant, so to my mind the name was a little unfortunate, but Allen appeared to be extremely fond of the man. It was Dettol said this and Dettol said that. In fact, Dettol seemed to be a right old know-it-all!

For our date, Allen chose a venue that was famous for its fondue, assuming that because I was from England, I must be a fondue expert. Huh? Despite his culinary ignorance, Allen was quite witty on the phone, and though he wasn't the first to say he loved my accent, he had the grace to say he knew I'd heard it a million times before.

Allen was very "into" European women, he told me. American women were uniformly brash and motivated only by money, he claimed—not like me. In fact, Allen wanted to take me to meet Dettol and his wife; he knew they would love me—as he did!

I knew things were moving along a little too quickly when he asked if I preferred penises circumcised or not. I decided to be honest with Allen and tell him that far from being my one-and-only, he was one in a thousand.

To my amazement, Allen loved the idea of being part of my quest, even asking if I would identify him by his full name, and if any European women wanted him, could I please give out his number? I agreed.

I never got to find out whether Allen was "cut or uncut," nor did we order any food. I left our date fondue-less, which was fine by me as I've always considered those fussy fondue sets a little too trendy for their own good. It's the kind of gift you get at Christmas and eventually give away to your child's bring-and-buy sale.

Much the same way I felt about Allen. ❤

With a name like Tarrow, I should have been alerted that there was something off about this man. He looked like Pee-wee Herman, and I soon saw that nothing about Tarrow was as it seemed. Here's what I learned:

- He was an office manager, but longed to be a ballroom dance teacher. He didn't go to dance classes, however, since he had no rhythm.
- He was an American, but would love to be European.
- Both his parents were alive, but he liked to tell people that he was an orphan because he thought it was romantic.

As it turns out, his name wasn't even Tarrow, of course, but Gregory. He had made up the name because it sounded "dramatic." He pointedly told me that the only reason he was meeting me was that it was "in and chic" to have a foreign girlfriend. He resorted to the personals because it was hard to find women who fully understood him. I would imagine he would have to search high, low, and in between to find someone who was on his very strange wavelength.

Tarrow guessed correctly that we wouldn't be having a second date, but he didn't feel it was a total loss. He described with delight how he would tell his coworkers that he had dined with a princess from England. Wouldn't that be something?

I could just imagine those poor people he worked with having to endure another episode of "The Tales of Tarrow." As we left, he bid me "Cheerio and ta ta" and asked that I say "a traditional English parting" in return. I said, "Good-bye, Tarrow." ❤

James, 41
Sales Director
SINGLE

In his message James said he could listen to me all day; even if I didn't want to meet him, could I please leave a message on his answering machine so he could hear my wonderful voice. (These people really need to get out more!) Well, flattery gets you everywhere, so I called him back.

James was so pleased I had called that he began to imitate the way I spoke. Unfortunately, like almost all Americans who try to do an English accent, it didn't sound like any part of England I've been to. (Now, I'm sure you all have other talents, but perfecting an English accent isn't one of them; I'm sure my American accent is just as bad.) I let it slide, though, and we arranged to meet for dinner.

James was eager to take me to his favorite restaurant, a real English pub. (This I had to see.) I got there before him and made my way to the bar, where I had a good laugh checking out the menu while waiting for him. Then James was at my side. He was of medium height with brown hair and a big smile, and as he shook my hand with both of his he asked if I'd had a "jolly good trip here." It turned out that James was a true Anglophile and couldn't wait to tell the barmaid that I was "really from England." She managed to contain her enthusiasm, replying, "Tally ho and all that shit!" before slapping down our Chardonnays.

James didn't seem to notice, so much in his element was he. He told me he brought all his dates here, although he wanted to reassure me that if we could meet here every evening he wouldn't date any other women. Would I promise him the same? I became engrossed in the menu right about then.

I had already taken stock of the "traditional English" fare offered by this establishment. In fact there was only one dish that was truly English: roast beef and Yorkshire pudding. You know what roast beef is, but in case you don't know about the pudding, let me enlighten you.

It's a batter, like pancake mixture, that's poured into a dish with a little meat juice, then baked in the oven until it rises and becomes crispy. Some people like to make individual puddings and then put the meat and gravy in them. (My mum wasn't above hiding brussels sprouts in there, too!) I've always been partial to Yorkshire pudding, and James urged me to try it, promising it was *so, so* good.

While we were waiting for this culinary delight to arrive, James begged me to tell him some real English sayings that he could use at work, spouting things like "Top of the morning to you" (that's Irish) and "By jove and all that" to get me going. I was rescued from this session with Professor Higgins by the arrival of our food—or so I thought. The highly touted Yorkshire pudding turned out to be a roll with the top sliced off. The inside had been scooped out and a blob of beef stew had been ladled into the cavity, then the top replaced at a somewhat jaunty angle. James tucked in like it was the Last Supper, making appreciative sounds as he ate.

Confused, I called the waitress over to ask what happened to the Yorkshire pudding. "It *is* Yorkshire pudding," she replied. When I looked dubious, she clarified, "It's *our* Yorkshire pudding."

Seeing my slightly aghast expression, James became embarrassed, having thought it was a truly authentic English meal he was wolfing down. I didn't want to hurt his feelings, so I ate my beef and bread without another word. In fact, from that point on James maintained a subdued silence as well.

At last it was time to go. James asked if we could swap some paper money and offered to trade me a dollar bill for a five-pound note, a deal that would have cost me about seven dollars. I suggested we split the check instead and offered my cheek for a kiss. He offered only a "Ta ta." ❤

Chris, 42
Manager of Printing Company
SINGLE

I met Chris for breakfast at a well-known local diner. He stood to greet me when I arrived and announced, "Wow, a real lady from England!" I turned to see who else was there; it had been quite some time since I'd been called a lady.

Chris was around five feet eight, and his slightly tubby body was encased in a blue uniform, as he had to be at work in an hour. He seemed to be in awe of me and I decided to make the most of it; after all, how often does someone think you're wonderful just because of where you were born? He asked me in all sincerity if I'd lived in a castle and whether I knew the Queen. I answered yes to both questions, hoping to put an end to that line of inquiry. No such luck!

He launched into an enthusiastic rendition of "Rule Britannia," waving his arms about in some sort of misguided gesture as he sang. The waitress brought our coffee over and looked at him and then me in bemused silence. Eventually she asked what we wanted to eat, and when Chris ordered his eggs he said, "Burn the British" (in Chris-speak this apparently meant he wanted a toasted English muffin). I wanted the ground to open up.

I kept the conversation flowing with tidbits of royal gossip, and when Chris asked if "it's true about Princess Fergie," I nodded, even though I had no idea what he was referring to. I didn't even go into the fact that she's not a princess anyway. As soon as I confirmed his suspicion, whatever it was, he grimaced, muttering, "I knew it, I knew it all the time."

As soon as was decently possible, I excused myself. Chris thanked me over and over for meeting him, and when I offered to pay the bill he agreed so long as he could keep the receipt as a souvenir.

Whatever you want, Chris. ♥

Peter, 45
Construction Worker
SINGLE

I had a good phone conversation with Peter, who seemed overjoyed that I had chosen him when I called. (I didn't feel the need to tell him my criteria.) We talked for quite a while and he was very witty and charming, so we arranged a date at an Irish bar. Peter himself claimed to be Irish, though he didn't have the Irish accent thing going on and he had no knowledge of Ireland, but what the heck.

At the bar, the barman (who wasn't Irish either) told me that the whole place had been imported from Ireland, piece by piece. Irish jokes were piped through in the bathroom, presumably so you could chuckle and pee at the same time. (That's not a bad name for a pub, don't you think? Welcome to the Chuckle and Pee!)

Peter told me he had been married twice and divorced twice, and though he loved women, he couldn't stay faithful to one person. He had been using the personal ads for about a year because women who place ads want sex and so did he. He had sunk quite a few Scotches by now, and he obviously felt emboldened because he looked me in the eye and asked me if I had any Irish in me. When I said no, he shot back, "Would you like some?" and cracked himself up. Apparently the barman thought it was pretty good too; with a leer he asked if I had any American in me and joined in Peter's lecherous laughter.

That was enough for me. I told Peter I had to leave and he very thoughtfully informed me he would be there every night should I wish to find him. About three weeks later he called the voicemail and said he didn't want a relationship with me, but he had liked my breasts and wondered how I would feel about having sex with him. I never called him back, so I assume he learned how I felt. Guess Peter just didn't have the luck of the Irish when it came to me. ❤

Jerry, 36
Production Technician
SINGLE

Jerry's sister had a best friend whose mother was from England, which in his mind practically made us old friends. He was a short, nice-looking man who appeared to love all things British and peppered me with questions about the royal family: Was Diana murdered? Is Fergie really a slut? (Fergie really does seem to be infamous to the Americans I was meeting.) What do I know? I only read the papers like everyone else. But I confirmed both, which pleased him no end.

After we reviewed his favorite Monty Python episodes, which he expected me to know (I didn't), we covered Benny Hill and the trip he hoped to make to London. He wanted to go but was concerned about the weather. I guess Jerry assumed all Brits walk about in the fog wearing black capes, or tapping canes along pavement with the hound of the Baskervilles wailing in the distance.

Through this all, Jerry was clearly so much in awe of me, it was weird. When he called his sister and asked me to say hello, though, it became embarrassing. She obviously didn't care who I was or where I was from. After we ate dinner, Jerry mentioned that this was the first time he had answered a personal ad, as he was quite a shy man. Tonight, apparently, all bets were off. Leaning forward conspiratorially, he confided that he had never fucked an Englishwoman before, but would like to. "It would be so proper," he gushed. Oh, and by the way, did I like to curse during sex? When I recovered from this abrupt change of face, I told him I liked to curse while I was having dinner with idiots like him, and he realized he'd gone a little too far. I then told him in no uncertain terms what I thought of him, throwing in a few choice curses for good measure. In retrospect he probably enjoyed that, but I was annoyed. For someone who started out all sweet and ever-so-happy-to-meet-you, he ended up an obnoxious pain in the you-know-what! ❤

Greg, 52
Lawyer
MARRIED

Greg was not just a lawyer; he was a lawyer who starred in his own TV commercials. His message told me to look out for him on a certain channel at such-and-such a time; if I liked what I saw, then I should call him. I had no hesitation in calling him because I had already seen said commercial and it was so sickly sweet, it was funny. You know the kind: a lawyer looking oh so sincere and caring, saying something along the lines of "If you have been injured or hurt at work, then call us and we'll take half your fat payoff!" It's amusing to me because in the U.K. lawyers are not allowed to tout for business as they are here.

When I called Greg, he said he felt honored that I had picked him. Once again, I felt no need to elaborate on my scientific method of selection, so we moved on to Greg's nationality. He told me he was French and was, in fact, quite knowledgeable on that country, although not its language.

We arranged to meet up later that evening at a restaurant, and he suggested I choose one of three places at which he had a regular table. I saw him as soon as I got out of the cab; he was at a table by the window, talking on a cell phone and writing on a napkin. I was shown to the table and my date stood and greeted me by kissing my hand without interrupting his phone conversation. As I waited for him to finish I looked down and noticed he wasn't wearing any socks. Very Don Johnson! At last he finished his conversation and he stretched both his arms out across the table and reached for my hands. "Forgive me, forgive me," he pleaded unctuously. Okay, a little over the top, but I remembered this man was a thespian of sorts. I even decided to overlook his propensity for calling me "darling" throughout our date.

He told me he had a very successful law practice and made a lot of money, but something was missing. The missing element? No, not his socks. Turns out he had no love in his life, despite the wife and a child waiting at home, and another baby on the way.

Nice. His wife is pregnant and he's scouring the personals in search of a bit on the side. We had a brief chat about me, and then he said, "Darling, would you like to spend the weekend with me? I have two days free. I could show you what this city is really all about." He seemed genuinely shocked when I declined his kind offer; apparently I was being very "un-European." (Does everyone from Europe cheat on their spouses?)

Undeterred, he asked if I would call him and I'm sure I will—if ever I am injured at work or ill-treated in a nursing home. Until then, I'll pass . . . darling. ❤

Colin, 36
Sales Assistant
SINGLE

This date had a real European connection. Colin was born in Manchester, England, and had lived there until he was five years old, when his family moved to America. He'd been there ever since. He asked if I would mind meeting him at his place of work for lunch and named a well-known discount store. No problem—I knew they had good chicken noodle soup, so at least I wouldn't go hungry.

Colin was waiting for me at the restaurant (cafeteria) and told me how pleased he was that I had actually turned up. His actual words were "Y'all came to ma jarb, ah'm gittin' real es-ahted."

He was medium height with light brown hair and was quite nice looking. It seems he had answered several ads previously and when he told the women where he worked, they either hung up the phone or didn't show up for the date. Perhaps, now that I was actually there, he decided to get all the bad news out of the way up front: He told me his penis was very small, even when he had an erection. Because of this he didn't like to have sex with anyone but himself.

This was far more information than I wanted or needed at this point, and I was a little unsure how to answer, though "Thanks for sharing" came to mind. (To have said "Women don't really care about size" would have been silly and I would have been lying, right?)

Colin obviously thought we would be getting intimate, and when I called him on it, sure enough, he did feel that as I had showed up to meet with him, when so many others had not, then surely on our next date we would have sex. After all, he was born in England—we had so much in common, raht?

I was amazed and I told him so, to which he replied, "Well, how many times do we have to git together before we *can* do it then?" I realized that this guy was not playing with a full deck, but as luck would have it I didn't have to answer. He heard his name called over the loudspeaker, requesting that he return to his section. He panicked and told me he'd "be rahrt bayack." I honestly did wait, until I had finished my chicken noodle soup anyway, and then I left before he got bayack. ❤

Sid, 56
Carpet Fitter
MARRIED

This date started with the most tenuous of European connections. Sid's neighbor Bill was from London, he told me; did I know him? As the population of London exceeds six million and Bill is not a particularly unusual name, I was not surprised that Sid's neighbor didn't ring any bells. But Sid loved all things English, and we did the Benny Hill / Monty Python, do-you-know-the-Queen bit for a few minutes.

We met up in an Italian restaurant for lunch, and Sid explained his reasons for wanting to meet me. He and his wife of thirty-five years didn't have a very good relationship anymore; she had got very fat, didn't care about her appearance, wouldn't have sex with him, and they hardly even spoke. He had been answering personal ads for six years and had placed his own ad but received no replies. None of the women he'd met throughout his six years of dating had come up to his standards; they were only after what they could get from him, he felt.

Now, without being rude, there was little that was attractive about this man. He could only be described as obese, his hygiene was poor, and his habit of cracking his knuckles was really annoying. But he had high standards and I guess there's nothing wrong with that (though there *is* something wrong with cheating on your wife). I couldn't even be bothered to find out why he and his wife didn't just go their separate ways, and I cut the date short when he said he needed sex so bad he thought his balls would burst. Frankly, I couldn't have cared if he had spontaneously combusted. ❤

Jim, 46
Interior Designer
MARRIED

Jim and his wife did lots of work for European families who had purchased homes in the States, and he "just loved" British women. They were "so sharp," and he had his eye on one or two whom he had made some window treatments for. Charming, I'm sure. These unsuspecting Brits call him in to measure their windows and he's sizing up the women instead.

Anyway, he asked if we could meet for lunch and I agreed. He told me he would mark me down in his diary as a customer, in case his wife should see. They worked together and she was a "scheming s.o.b." (*she* was?) so he had to play it safe. If by chance she should call me, he asked that I pretend to be having an estimate done on a master bedroom. I told him I didn't give out my home phone number, but wondered what I should say if by chance she called the voicemail service, which he didn't find funny.

He had told me that I'd know him by his "sharp" yellow shirt, and I certainly did. He was sitting at a table mangling the lyrics to a Bob Marley song as I approached him, and when I asked if he was Jim, he said, "No, I'm not." As I made to walk away he pulled my arm and said, "Yes I'm Jim, ha ha ha ha!" Oh dear, a comedian.

Over drinks Jim told me about the cute Englishwomen that he'd done work for. He loved their accents and the way they would ask him if he wanted a "cuppa tea," and though he hadn't actually had sex with any of them yet, he would like to. However, he really only wanted sex and he was concerned that they might want more from him.

To be perfectly honest, I sincerely doubted they'd want even that much. Jim was a very plain man with wiry gray hair and much of it sprouting out of his nose. He had mopped his face with a tissue, and half of it was still on his face while the other half was being used to staunch a bleeding gum. From time to time he would investigate how much blood was on the tissue, then back it went into his mouth.

I asked if he thought that answering my ad was wrong since, after all, he was a married man. At this, Jim got scared and asked if I was "on a mission." I decided to be a comedian, too, and told him someone who thought he needed to be taught a lesson had sent me. He jumped up, knocking over his chair in the process, and ran off.

I wonder how he feels about British women now? ❤

Edward, 36
Waiter
SINGLE

I had great difficulty hearing Edward's message over the loud music blaring in the background, but he was caller number three so I had to give him a call. There was still loud music playing when he answered, and he kept yelling, "What, can't hear ya" into the phone.

As it turned out we were not that far away from each other and we decided to do lunch that very day. We hadn't even ordered entrées when Edward launched into his great love for Queen—not the monarch, but the rock group. He was a real die-hard fan, it seemed, and the worst day of his life was when Freddie Mercury died. He recited his favorite songs and albums and was shocked and appalled that I wasn't particularly partial to Mr. Mercury and company.

It soon became apparent that the only reason he wanted to meet me was to see if I could get him some Queen memorabilia from London. He named a couple of shops that he had read about and I promised I would check them out for him, which made him so happy that he commenced strumming an air guitar to the accompaniment of noises that could only be described as "downg de downg downg downg."

Edward had to rush off to work and I was not too upset about that. He told me where he worked and said I was welcome any time. That was nice. We really had nothing in common but at least he wasn't cheating on his wife or girlfriend, so that made him okay in my (this) book. As a reward, I put someone in touch with Edward so he could purchase his precious Queen stuff. ❤

Steve, 36
Driver
MARRIED

Occasionally I heard from true Europeans looking for a taste of home. Steve was an Englishman living in Florida. He'd been there for four years and loved it, he said. The only problem was his wife: She didn't like America and wanted to go home to Norfolk. He said she was a bit strange and I believed him; how anyone can prefer a dismal town like Norfolk to Miami, I do not know. But who am I to judge?

Steve seemed like a nice man to talk to, but of course he wasn't, as he was attempting to be unfaithful. And like so many other men, he thought it was absolutely fine to speak about his wife and, in the next breath, ask for sex.

We had a pleasant hour chatting about England, so I was a bit taken aback when he asked if we could go to a hotel, as he was feeling "orny." I told him to go tell his wife and we chatted on some more, which was quite odd after such a personal proposition. Steve revealed that the only time he went back to England was when he needed to see a doctor, as he didn't have insurance in the U.S. Then he showed me his corns and a bunion wrapped in a Band-Aid and said he would have to make a trip back home soon to get them sorted out. Bunions over lunch was even more intimate than Steve's sexual come-on, and I beat a hasty retreat before he started discussing any more personal tidbits.

Sex, wives, and bunion tape. What more can a girl ask for? ❤

Craig, 42
Computer Technician
SINGLE

I met Craig at a Pizza Hut. He had initially asked me to come to his house so he could cook me a meal, but understood when I said I would rather not. He mentioned that his mother's mother was from Nottingham in the north of England and that he would be wearing jeans and a white shirt.

When I walked into the place, right on time, I saw him hunkered over the salad bar. He'd obviously decided not to wait for me. I waited until he went back to the table and walked over to introduce myself. He wiped salad dressing from his mouth with his hand and then offered the same hand for me to shake, announcing, "I've ordered us a pizza, but I didn't know what you wanted to drink." He didn't know what I wanted on my pizza either, or if I may have preferred pasta, but I said a diet soda would be fine, which prompted him to snarl, "I hope you're not one of those diet fiends. I can't stand women who don't eat. Order a proper drink for God's sake."

This wasn't just good-natured jibing—he looked really angry. He went on to say I was "skinny as a rat" and I should "get with it and eat!" Oddly, I found I'd suddenly lost my appetite, and made an excuse to get out of there.

After all the men I'd met who had justified their infidelities by blaming their wives' ever-ballooning weight, I should have found this a pleasant change of pace, but somehow I didn't.

And by the way, I like pepperoni on my pizza. ❤

"Pretentious" doesn't begin to describe Marcus. His message was peppered with references to the four years he'd spent in London and other places he'd visited, and he name-dropped far too many names for my liking. But you know the rules. . . .

"Well, well, well," he said when we finally spoke, "my English friend has called." He couldn't speak for long, but we arranged a date for the following day. He asked if I liked Italian food and said he'd make the reservations. With a lordly "*Ciao*," he was gone.

Marcus and I arrived at exactly the same time, or so I thought. As we sat down, he told me that he had been standing across the street, waiting to size me up. If I had been a "freaking mess," he confided, he would have beat it. Well, apparently I passed muster, and so did he, at least physically, though his manner was something else altogether.

He talked a lot about himself, and when I made appreciative murmurs of encouragement he smiled and said, "You do speak this language of ours well, don't you?"

Marcus then asked if I knew how to eat spaghetti "in the proper way."

I decided to humor this condescending twit and said I would like his help with my food. He was only too happy to oblige, and when the meal arrived he ostentatiously showed me how to twist the pasta onto my fork using the spoon as a helper (which Italians, at least adult Italians, never do). I pretended to listen and learn, and leaned forward to accept the pasta into my mouth, which Marcus assured me was okay to do when you ate spaghetti. I was only grateful I hadn't ordered lobster; imagine all the lessons to be learned there!

Luckily Marcus had an appointment that he couldn't get out of, but as we prepared to leave the restaurant, he asked me how I felt about sushi. I actually hate sushi, but as I didn't plan to see him again, there didn't seem to be any point in furnishing him with that information. He asked for my home number and became a little upset when I wouldn't give it to him. Then he asked that I not meet any more men because he felt we "had something"! It was easier to go along with him than to argue or question him. He "*Ciao*'d" everyone in the restaurant and then he kissed me on both cheeks and we said good-bye.

I still can't make out what it was Marcus thought we'd "got," but whatever it is, I don't want any of it! ❤

Donald, 41
Construction Worker
SINGLE

Donald loved England and everything about it, though he'd never visited. (In fact he had never ventured outside the state of Florida.) But he was a huge fan of the English television program *Are You Being Served,* which is shown on PBS. If you've never seen the show, it's set in a department store and the central characters include a forty-year-old gay man who minces around trilling "I'm free" and a pink-haired fifty-five-year-old sales assistant who refers to her cat as "my pussy." All right, it can be funny, but the show is twenty years old and is definitely not reality programming (sorry to disappoint you, Donald). Over lunch he talked about particular episodes that were among his favorites; he told me he taped as many shows as he could and played them over and over. I believed him—he could recite whole chunks verbatim. But after a while, I told him I had to go. I was stupefied with boredom, and anyway, I had to go and feed *my* pussy. ❤

Voitek, 44
Tailor
MARRIED

This man's European connection was to Poland. He certainly had a strong accent, and his name was Polish too. He had been living in America for thirty years and although he loved it, he visited Poland every year, as did his parents. He expressed how "pleased" he was that I was English and was even more pleased when I told him I had visited Poland. In fact he was pleased about everything.

I wasn't too pleased with his choice of meeting place, though. I was the only female there, and it was full of men smoking cigarettes and speaking Polish. We ordered schnitzel and mashed potatoes for our dinner—and I must tell you that it was the most delicious meal, so the evening wasn't a total loss. Alas, Voitek and I never really made a connection; he said he'd never "read advertisements for ladies before" but a man who works for him had told him it was a fine way to meet women. I asked why he wanted to meet ladies if he was married, and he just laughed and coughed at the same time.

I declined his offer of a drink at a bar where we could "drink plenty, plenty vodka" and thanked him for a lovely meal. He gave me his cell phone number, then admitted it was never on as he didn't know how to use it. I left to the sound of his coughing and laughing and went off to get plenty, plenty fresh air. *Dowidzenia,* Voitek. (That's good-bye.) ❤

Marty, 43
Furniture Warehouse Owner
MARRIED

Marty had seen my ad in the paper while waiting for a plane. He'd only answered one ad before, and it had been a disaster. However, that date had been three years ago, so he'd decided to give mine a go.

The message he left on my voicemail was quite informative. He admitted he was married and said he'd elaborate on that when we met. (Sure of himself, wasn't he?) His European connection was his Scottish spouse; he had also been to Europe and loved it, so he "knew" he would love me too.

We arranged a date for lunch.

On the appointed day, I sat in a restaurant that was vacant save for a single waiter. I'd been nursing a glass of wine for half an hour when a large, red-faced man came bursting in, wearing spandex shorts and a designer T-shirt. Marty apologized for his tardiness, explaining that he'd taken his wife to the doctor's office. She wasn't sick; she was having collagen injections in her lips! We exchanged a few pleasantries, but then he said that I should try to gain a little weight; real men (like Marty) like something to hold on to, apparently.

Over appetizers, Marty stressed to me that he would not leave his wife under any circumstances. I had to make it very clear to *him* that I had no intention of asking him to leave his wife—he was way ahead of me! When he began to fiddle about with his spandex-clad private parts, I knew it was time to go.

I thanked Marty for meeting me, but told him we wouldn't be meeting again. He picked up his keys and his cell phone and made for the door as if trying to beat me to the exit. He called back to me that I was too skinny anyway and he didn't want to see me again either. The waiter was hovering about with the check, obviously afraid that we were about to "do a runner," and as I paid he commented that the man was "bery, bery rude." I agreed that he was. As I glanced out the window, I could see that Marty was standing by a car fiddling about with his penis through his shorts. In fact, he was kneading it like a baker making bread! I asked the waiter if there was another way out, and he showed me the exit through the kitchen. I thanked him "bery" much and went home. ❤

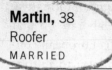

Martin, 38
Roofer
MARRIED

Martin was an Englishman visiting the States on holiday, so it seemed strange that he'd answered a personal ad. He wasn't familiar with the area, so I chose a restaurant. I was there for twenty-five minutes before he arrived (and I wouldn't have waited that long except that the couple at the next table was having a huge row and I wanted to see how it ended). When he eventually got there, Martin was wearing the regulation uniform for British tourists: black socks and sneakers, navy blue shorts, and a shirt that he would normally wear to work. He was of course crimson with sunburn, and wore a fanny pack around his hips. Very attractive indeed!

Martin confessed that he was on vacation with his wife and two kids. He'd dropped them off at one of the local attractions and feigned tiredness so he could meet up with me. "The wife" was expecting him to pick them up for dinner, so he couldn't eat with me or she might suspect something. It was clear that he thought he was enormously clever, getting away from his wife this way. His reasons for straying, though, couldn't have been more banal: They hadn't been getting along for some time and he only stayed for the kids' sake. I had heard that stupid phrase so many times from so many men that I almost said it along with him. I sent him back to the Magic Kingdom, with his tail between his legs. ❤

weirdos, wackos, and a deviant or two
(hold on tight— this is going to be a long chapter!)

I knew I would meet some strange men—not because I was in America but because of the sheer number of men I was meeting. By the law of averages, if you meet a hundred people, one or two of them may be a sandwich short of a picnic. But this lot was not just a sandwich short, they were missing the basket, blanket, and all the ants! My dates divulged the wildest sexual fantasies and the craziest turn-ons. I lost count of the times I wanted to laugh out loud when told by the complete stranger sitting opposite me that he liked to have his bottom tickled with the heel of a stiletto shoe. Or he just adored wearing toddler clothes and being called a sissy boy. If the fifty-six-year-old man who smirked "Nice legs honey, wouldn't mind them around my neck" reads this, I hope he cringes as much as I did when he said it. I almost choked on my food when a date asked if I had ever had a rather sensitive part of my anatomy nailed to a table.

Then there were the guys in women's underwear and the oddballs who couldn't perform any sexual act without having various food items smeared about their private parts. Lots of them were married but had wives who didn't want to participate in their antics, and the single guys were always looking for a like-minded female to play with. Both married and single men told me that the more women they met, the more likely they were to find someone who shared their very peculiar passion, or would at least go along with it—hence their penchant for the personals.

As for myself, though, I can't get my head around the fact of a grown man who wants to wear baby clothes or dress up in women's clothes with a full face of makeup. I really like a man to be a man. What was clear as day, however, was that no amount of revulsion—or hilarity—will deter these men from seeking out willing partners, so caveat emptor.

Max, 34
Realtor
MARRIED

I was already at the restaurant when I saw Max pull up in his black Porsche. His blond hair was tied back in a ponytail and though it was 8 P.M., he wore sunglasses. He apologized for being late and sat down opposite me, remarking that I had nice nails. I thanked him and we ordered drinks and some food.

Before either arrived, Max had begun telling me private and intimate things about his wife. It seems that he'd paid to have her breasts enlarged twice, and though he'd given her everything she wanted, she still wouldn't do what Max liked. His request? For a woman to "toss his salad." Without getting too specific,

I'll tell you this has nothing to do with lettuce, tomato, or mayonnaise. I'll spare the details except to say that salad tossing was a sexual quirk that Max liked very much and his wife liked not at all. When he explained to me what it was, I came down on the side of the wife and I asked him why he would tell me, a stranger, something so personal. He shrugged and explained that there was always the chance I might like it too, and if not, so what? No one would ever know. (Ha ha, Max, that's what you think!) Poor woman, maybe her twice-enlarged breasts were so big now that she couldn't get near the salad. ❤

Joel, 38
Sales Director
MARRIED

When I called Joel, he said that he had a particular fetish he would describe to me when we met. I could hardly wait. He described himself as "very good looking, handsome, and attractive." All of those things? We arranged to meet the following day for lunch, and I must tell you that Joel was none of the above. In fact, he was quite ordinary to look at. We shook hands, and moments after we were shown to our table Joel told me what he had in mind.

He said he would like me to find him on a bed in a hotel room, fully clothed in a business suit but barefoot. My role was to tie him up on the bed and tickle his feet. I asked what I would get out of the arrangement and Joel admitted that he hadn't really thought about that. In fact he seemed confused that I wasn't interested. Finally he suggested he could tickle me too. I still said thanks but no thanks, whereupon he announced he wouldn't pay for my drink if I was going to be rude. He had thought I would be different from American women, but I turned out to be just as ignorant.

I'm glad to know that I'm in the same category as the ignorant American females who turned this creep down. ❤

Brian told me on the phone that he was six feet tall, with blond hair and blue eyes. He said that the company he owned was doing quite well and that he now had six employees. He made good money, had a boat, and liked to go sailing. From our conversation, he sounded like a great catch.

Over dinner at his favorite Chinese restaurant, Brian asked if he could be open and honest with me. I was sure he was going to confess that he was wearing women's underwear. I was ready for him.

But I had got it wrong. Brian said he had baby-doll fantasies. I was unsure of how to react since I wasn't sure what he meant.

He elaborated. During foreplay, he liked to dress up like a baby doll. He had all the clothes and equipment that a baby doll needs. Oh, and did I mention that Brian liked to be a female baby doll?

I wondered what possessed a builder, a strapping six-footer, to dress up like a baby girl. He said, "Sometimes you just like to do things and you don't have a reason. Hasn't that ever happened to you?"

It was hard for him to find a woman who enjoyed his fantasy, or even understood it. He had once had a girlfriend who would indulge him and they'd had great fun. Brian was the baby doll and she was the mommy. Where was she now? I asked. They'd split up and she was now married to a reverend!

I wanted to laugh, but he was so sincere about being a "baby doll" that I didn't want to hurt his feelings. When he told me he had his "best erections ever" wearing baby dresses, though, I'm afraid I lost it! As soon as I regained my composure, I apologized. But I had apparently ruined the date. Brian had been looking for someone to be his mommy just occasionally, not every time we met. He had money and we could have had a good time, if only I had been willing to role-play once in a while. He wasn't mad at me, he said, just "very disappointed."

I didn't know what to say to make him feel better. "Goodbye" was probably best. Before he left, Brian shook my hand and said, "You would have been a good mommy, I know it."

I know I was, and am, a good mommy . . . to my son! Certainly not to a grown man who climbs up on roofs by day and dons baby clothes when the sun goes down! Baby-doll Brian? I've left you an orphan! ❤

Derek, 38
Lawyer
SINGLE

Derek had left a very detailed voice-mail message, and when we met up, I felt as though I knew a lot about him. As it turned out, there were a few things he hadn't mentioned on the phone.

We met for our lunch date at a very nice seafood restaurant on Miami Beach. Derek was dressed in an Armani suit with Armani shades and a white Armani vest. When we had been seated at a table in the corner, Derek informed me that he had a "rock in his pocket" and it was hurting him. I told him to take it out, then.

"Really, you wanna see it?" he asked.

I told him I didn't particularly want to see it, but if it was causing him pain, then he should take it out. He smiled at me and said, "Oh, I knew that British women were horny, but baby you are making me so hard."

He scooted his chair back from the table and said, "Look at what you've done to me! I need to go to the bathroom, but I can't go like this. I'll be arrested!"

Finally the light dawned. I took a quick look in the direction of his Armani-clad privates and told him that I couldn't see anything. With that, I picked up my bag (which wasn't Armani) and headed for the door, leaving Derek gazing at his groin. ❤

Richard, 44
Chiropractor
MARRIED

Initially, when I listened to Richard's message, I thought he was a regular guy. Okay, he was married, but apart from that he didn't say anything even mildly strange. He described himself as a "creative and happy" male, of medium build, attractive, and with a full head of hair.

When I set off to meet him at the designated venue, I figured that if all else failed I could tell Richard about my disc problems, so at least there wouldn't be any long silences.

At the restaurant I was shown to a table, where Richard was waiting. First impressions were favorable. He'd been honest about his looks. He was drinking a Bellini and ordered me a glass of Champagne. Very swish indeed! Richard asked about me, what I liked to do in my spare time, all very normal first-date stuff.

Maybe it was the three Bellinis he'd quaffed, but after a while Richard obviously felt it was time to move the conversation to subjects of a more personal nature. He ordered a fourth drink, then announced, "I am straight. You won't find a man more straight than me." Had I asked if he was gay? I'd only had two drinks and I was sure I hadn't questioned Richard's sexuality. I guessed that Richard probably had a fantasy involving another man, and now he was worried that he might be bisexual. Wrong.

It seemed Richard liked to dress his penis up like a beauty queen. He explained how he would put Barbie clothes on his willy and act out beauty pageants. At this point I burst out with laughter. I just couldn't help myself. The image of male genitals clad in Barbie outfits was too much. Besides, what would Ken say?

I did apologize for laughing, and he said that he expected me to have been "a little more understanding. After all," he added, "you're from England. Where's that British reserve we always hear about?"

I tried hard not to smile and told him that he had to admit it would strike most people, English or not, as very funny. He glared at me, signifying that our date was over.

"You have made fun of me," he said as I rose. I didn't bother to tell him, as he waved his hand to dismiss me, that he had done very well on his own. ❤

Simon, 39
Engineer
MARRIED

Simon told me that he and his wife had an open marriage, and she knew that he was answering my ad. I didn't believe it, but I went to meet him anyway.

I liked the way he looked. Simon was a striking man, fairly tall, with brown hair and eyes. Although he wore glasses, I could see that he had beautiful eyes.

We had met at a restaurant, and as I was tucking into my Caesar salad, Simon asked if I smoked. I told him I did not. Then he asked, "Would you just hold a cigarette in your mouth, without inhaling?" Oh, that old one? When I asked why, Simon told me that he liked to massage women's feet while they smoked. His wife didn't smoke, and she had sensitive feet, so she was no good. It was just Simon's luck that I, too, hate to have my feet touched.

"Oh," he said, "well, that's my thing. I can't do it unless I can go through that process first." When I demurred, he tried to convince me by saying "You only have to sit there and smoke. I'll do the rest." It sounded harmless, if unappetizing, but really I didn't want to be there any longer. I could tell he didn't want me there either, because he was looking at his watch and signaling for the check. Simon said he was sorry, but he had to go. I wasn't sorry at all. ❤

Norman, 29
Salesman
SINGLE

Norman mentioned on the phone that he liked women with long hair. Quite how *much* he liked them wasn't apparent until we met. We had arranged a meeting during our conversation, and in the days leading up to our date Norman called three times to confirm. The appointed day was extremely windy, and when I arrived I went straight to the ladies' room to tidy my hair. I took it down from a ponytail and brushed it through. For some reason, I decided not to tie it back again. Fatal error.

Norman was waiting at the bar, drinking a beer. He smiled at me and as I sat down beside him, he took a handful of my hair and twisted it around his hand, the way you would wind wool, until his fingers were touching my head. I asked him to stop, and he did, but he told me he *loved* long hair. In fact, he loved it so much he wanted to eat it. Eat my hair? Yes, he said, chew it and swallow it. Norman loved to twist hair around his fingers, and then bite it off and have it for a snack. Wasn't eating hair bad for him? I asked. He agreed that it was, and said he would sometimes vomit and choke. That, he confided, was part of the turn-on.

I didn't want, or need, to hear any more from the hair-snacker, so I finished my wine and made an excuse to leave. Norman accepted my decision gracefully, but as I got up he asked if I had any hair in my brush that he could have for later on. I refused him that pleasure. As I left, I wondered how much hair a person could eat before they would become very sick. I think Norman was past his limit; he seemed to me pretty ill already. ❤

David, 41
Furniture Salesman
MARRIED

David told me that he used to be a baseball player. To be honest, I know so little about baseball that he could have told me he was Babe Ruth and I would have believed him.

Anyway, he sounded nice enough on the phone (though I haven't forgotten that he's a married man; I never forget!), so we arranged to meet for lunch. David said, "I have a platinum card and I go for quantity, not quality." That was a bit of a contradiction, wasn't it? David then named our venue: the cafeteria of a major discount warehouse. Seems he was a platinum member of . . . Costco!

I arrived at noon, flashed my card at the entrance (hey, I'm a member too), and headed towards the pretzel machine we'd designated as our meeting place. I knew David by sight when he approached, as he was wearing a shirt with his company's name on the pocket. At the food counter, I had a choice of pizza, hot dogs, or a burger. David recommended the pizza, and I went along with his suggestion.

As we took our food to a table, David confided that he always ate there because the food was good and very cheap. He didn't believe in paying more than five dollars for a meal. When I asked David why he had answered my ad, he said that he had just wanted someone to chat with on his lunch break. He had some problems that he wanted to discuss with someone who didn't know him or his family. In return, he would buy them lunch! As he spoke, he smiled as if he had just offered me the world, not a slice of pepperoni pizza, and only a fool would refuse. He leaned towards me and said, "It could be worse. I'm a nice guy and we could make this a regular thing. What do you think?" I didn't really want to tell him what I was thinking, so instead I told him that I didn't have time to be his unpaid counselor and we wouldn't be meeting again. David became a bit miffed at that, and he told me that he didn't like to be taken for a ride. He asked to be reimbursed for my lunch, all $4.79 of it. I gave him ten dollars and told him I had no problem paying for his lunch too, as the food had been fine. The company, however, was something else. ❤

Michael, 39
Investment Banker
SINGLE

Michael described himself as six feet three, of medium build, and quite handsome. We agreed to meet up for drinks in a place he knew. When I checked the voicemail later on that day, Michael was there again, asking me to please call him. I guessed he wanted to cancel or reschedule our date, but he had another agenda. He wanted to know if I had any children. When I told him I had a son, he sounded disappointed, but when I said he was sixteen, he brightened up. Very strange. When I asked why he needed to know this, Michael said he was "just curious."

I met him at the designated venue. He greeted me warmly, as if we were old friends, and complimented me on my hair. I thanked him and we ordered some wine. When the waiter moved away from our table, Michael told me he would like to speak to me openly. I began to try to guess what he was about to confess. Was he really married and looking to cheat? Did he like to be spanked, or to wear women's underwear?

No, Michael was an "adult baby" who was looking for

someone to be his "mommy." He was really hoping to meet a woman who was childless—hence his question to me about children. But as my son was older, perhaps I might like to play the "mom and baby" role again. He couldn't be serious . . . but of course he was.

I had to ask why this idea was so appealing to him, an obviously successful, confident man. Michael explained that babies have nothing to worry about other than being fed and diapered. He, on the other hand, had mountains of stress and worry in his life. Being a baby took all his cares away. As he warmed to his subject, he even admitted how he loved to wear baby clothes and lie in his "mommy's" arms. I envisioned the very big "mommy" that would be needed to cradle this huge baby. He continued on, telling me that he'd found an old Silver Cross pram in which he would lie to relax.

Michael eventually realized this scene wasn't for me. He said he figured he'd have to keep using prostitutes for his fantasy until he found a woman who wanted him as her baby. We said our good-byes, and Michael got up to leave. I watched as he went to the door. More than one woman gave him the once-over. I wondered if any were quite maternal enough. ❤

Paul, 40
Photographer
SINGLE

On the phone Paul sounded pretty normal, mentioning that he'd had a few dates from the personals but things hadn't quite worked out with any of them. Being a photographer was demanding work and he traveled a lot, so he used ads as a way of meeting women. At the time, the explanation seemed perfectly plausible.

When we met up, however, I quickly realized that Paul was one very strange man. After ordering us some drinks, he turned to me and asked, "Have you ever had the urge to speak without using the first letter of each word?"

He took my bemused silence as a cue to demonstrate exactly what he meant: "O ou ike t ere?" That, he explained, was "Do you like it here?" He went on: "Ow ou oing?" Obviously that was "How you doing?" I was beginning to get the hang of this. But what was the point of this ridiculous exercise?

Paul pressed on, urging me to try it. When I declined to order the next round of drinks in his wacky language, he looked hurt and said I was being childish. He's talking gibberish and I'm the child?

My lack of enthusiasm didn't deter Paul from calling the waiter over and trying to order the drinks in this inane way. The poor man was completely baffled and clearly thought my date had a serious speech impediment. The wordplay that had started out as mildly amusing was now bordering on bloody asinine, so I called the waiter over to bring the check. The poor thing looked scared as he approached our table, no doubt wondering what verbal diarrhea was about to spout forth.

I paid up and bid Paul good-bye. He sat slouched in his chair and didn't look up as he said, "Ood ye."

Yeah, Paul. Ood iddance. ❤

Gus, 40
Designer
SINGLE

Gus had an extremely deep voice, and when I returned his call, he insisted on calling me "Darrrling" and said that he wanted to take me to dinner right that minute! I suggested we meet instead at the same time the next day. That was agreed, and he named a restaurant on the Upper East Side that I'd never heard of. When I got there, two attendants took my coat and I was almost danced across the floor to a table where Gus awaited me. "Darrrling, you're here," he growled. The attendants sat me down, pushed my chair in, then stood at the opposite end of the table and smiled. I smiled back and they smiled back, and if Gus hadn't ordered Champagne we might all have carried on grinning away all night. Possibly not a bad option in light of the revelation that followed.

Gus warned me that I might not be into his scene, but he wanted to try anyway. I laid bets with myself that he was going to tell me he was wearing women's underwear, given his penchant for nice things and refined surroundings, so I was surprised when he had a more risqué scenario in mind.

Gus said he'd love for me to take him deep into the woods. Once there, I'd put him over my knee, pull down his pants to reveal no underwear, and then spank him with an expensive high-heeled shoe. We'd be caught in the act by a girlfriend of mine (just passing by, I guess) who happened to have a camera. We'd take all kinds of erotic photos of him posing with each of us. At the end of this rather improbable scenario Gus sat back and said, "Darrrling, is that hot or what?" He didn't wait for an answer, telling me instead that he had met several women from personal ads who had all been willing to go along with this fantasy. Now he'd tired of them and wanted someone new.

In no uncertain terms I told him, "Gus, I am not running around in Dolce & Gabbana heels in the mud with a friend so you can get your rocks off. And on top of it all, you'll soon be bored with me and scouring the ads for someone new. All I'll have is very sore knees and a hell of a job getting the mud off my heels. Thanks but no thanks . . . darrrling." His face darkened and he said that I'd mocked him. He looked at his watch and said he had to leave. He shook my hand and thanked me for meeting him, and two attendants came and danced him out the door.

After he'd left the attendants came over and presented me with the bill, but just as I was picking it up, Gus swooped back in. He picked up the bill and said, "I'll get this. I won't have you saying I'm a cheap bastard." He left, clutching the bill self-righteously, and I could assure him that I'd never call him cheap. ❤

Victor, 41
Real Estate Salesman
MARRIED

I knew immediately from Victor's message that he was going to be an oddball. Not that I was being exceptionally perceptive—Victor all but told me he was a little crispy round the edges. His message was fairly informative: He described himself in detail, then went on to list all his preferred activities, which ranged from snow skiing and horseback riding to "finger dancing." When I called him back, I asked exactly what "finger dancing" was, and Victor was thrilled that I had expressed interest in his "real passion." He wanted to meet me then and there, and said he would cancel all appointments so we could go for lunch. Maybe we could even stay on for dinner!

When I arrived, Victor was waiting for me at the bar. And a nice-looking man he was, too. As I sat beside him sipping my wine, however, I couldn't help noticing that he had Band-Aids on all his fingers except the thumbs. I was dying to get to the "finger dancing" part of this date, and as soon as we were shown to our table, Victor asked if he could demonstrate. I agreed without hesitation. This I wanted to see.

To the beat of an old Boomtown Rats tune (he really preferred reggae, but no matter), Victor twisted and twirled his fingers around on the table. He continued to "finger-dance" to all the tunes that the restaurant played, and when a Bob Marley song came on, he was in his element. His fingers were dipping and twisting all over the table, and I promise you that by the time the record had finished playing, we had a crowd around our table. I know this makes me sound as strange as he, but if you looked only at his fingers, it really did look like little legs dancing!

I praised Victor's dexterity, and he told me that occasionally he dressed his fingers up in special "finger shoes" and entered competitions. Lest I be tempted to join him in a tabletop tango, Victor took a look at my fingers and observed that my nails were much too long for serious dancing. His solo status didn't deter him from finger dancing throughout our entire meal, offering little finger bows to acknowledge the applause from our fascinated audience. The only time he stopped was to eat, and even then he was twiddling his fingers while holding the fork.

I tried to have a normal conversation with Victor, though it was a bit difficult for me to be serious after all that dancing. I asked why he was dating since he was a married man, and he told me that his wife had absolutely no interest in his finger dancing; in fact, she thought he was crazy! He would have liked to leave her but his real estate license was with her father's brokerage firm, so he stayed.

He seemed pathetically grateful that I liked what I had seen and said he hoped that we might meet up again. He graciously offered to pick up the check, and although I was grateful for that, I balked at his request that I kiss each of his fingers for luck (he had a big competition at the end of the month). Instead of ten kisses, I wished him ten times the best of luck. ❤

Clyde, 37
Textile Designer
SINGLE

If Clyde had mentioned his fascination with Saran Wrap on the phone, I doubt we would have made a date. (Actually, given my generous dating parameters, who knows?) We met for lunch at a very nice Tex-Mex bar. After ten minutes he casually asked, "Do you like Saran Wrap?" I was a little confused by the question but allowed as how I did use Saran Wrap for my leftovers, so I guessed I did like it. He smiled at this response and probed further. Did I like the *feel* of Saran Wrap? Oh, *now* I get it. To cut a long date short, Clyde revealed that he liked to wrap his penis in plastic wrap and ejaculate into a ball of wrap that he'd made earlier. What did he find exciting about that? He didn't know. He just liked it, he said, smiling with a bit of embarrassment.

Where did I fit in with all this wrapping? It was Clyde's hope that I would want to watch while he did his thing and even join in, if I desired. I didn't.

That about wrapped up our date, so to speak, and I thanked Clyde for meeting me and offered to pay my share. He refused to accept my money, but asked if I would give him my home number so he could call me later on while he was wrapping up his penis. I couldn't think of a single reason why I would want to listen to that. Undeterred, he said, "Can I do it to your answering machine, then?"

No, Clyde, and that's a wrap. ❤

Kieran, 36
Wholesale Furniture Company Owner
MARRIED

When I spoke with Kieran on the phone, he asked how I liked Glenn Miller, treating me to a bit of "In the Mood" by going "De de de de de de deeedee de de de de de de deeeeeedee." I told him my knowledge of Mr. Miller didn't go much beyond the song "Pennsylvania 6-5000" and I wasn't even completely sure if that was him. He was clearly disappointed but rallied enough to suggest that we meet up for dinner at a hotel that hosted a 1940s revival night. It was a novel idea, so I accepted. Just before I hung up, he asked my dress size. I thought this was his sneaky way of trying to find out if I was a large lady, but his ulterior motive was entirely different.

When I arrived for our rendezvous, I was shown to a table where a gentleman decked out in 1940s military garb—from capped head to gleaming black-toed shoes—awaited. He introduced himself to me as "Major Keiran Harrison at your service, ma'am." It was all terribly authentic, though I was painfully aware that no one else in the place was dressed in period attire. Before I could sit down, he handed me a gift box. I opened it, thinking it was a large box of chocolates, but amid all the tissue paper lay a silky blue dress. I could picture Hedy Lamarr wearing something just like it. He was so happy that I was petite; he just *knew* the dress would look divine on me. I thanked him but declined the gift. Now he was less pleased but still hopeful, and as I was still standing, Kieran asked if he could at least draw a line up the back of my legs to make it look as though I was wearing seamed stockings. Time out, Kieran!

Acknowledging defeat, he asked me to sit down and suggested we talk about Glenn Miller's death. (If I had a nickel for every date that went off on *that* tangent . . .) Kieran wanted to discuss the fact that the plane Glenn Miller was in had gone down in the English Channel. I tried to explain that I didn't know enough about Glenn Miller or his death fifty-odd years ago, and I really didn't want to participate in his wartime fantasies. Petulantly, Kieran said, "Then you can't have the gift I brought for you." More clothing? No, this was a genuine Bakelite telephone, and he took great pleasure in letting me know that it was no longer on offer. With that he announced, "You are dismissed." 💙

Enzo, 40
Unemployed
SINGLE

Enzo was one of the few truly scary weirdos I met. Arriving about fifteen minutes late for our date at a small Italian restaurant, he gave me a big hug and suggested we sit side by side. I said I'd feel more comfortable if we sat opposite one another. (Little did I know how right I was.)

After looking furtively around the restaurant, Enzo blurted out that someone was out to get him, even trying to kill him, and that's why he was wearing a bulletproof vest and carrying a gun in his sock. Then he went into the various activities that put him in such a precarious situation. In the first ten minutes of our date he'd spoken about drugs, guns, pornography, and hookers. Charming, especially if any of it was true. I told him I had to go to the ladies' room. I just didn't tell him it was the ladies' room at a department store six blocks away. 💙

Martin, 34
Telephone Sales
MARRIED

When we spoke on the phone, Martin sounded pleasant enough. But I, of all people, should have known that things aren't always what they seem. He told me that if he could eat at my house, he'd bring the food with him. I said I'd rather not do that, as we didn't know each other, and suggested that we meet in mutual territory. Martin said, "Can you give me directions? I don't know where that is." He wasn't joking, but he had the grace to be a little embarrassed when I explained the meaning of "mutual territory." He had thought it was a restaurant.

It was quite chilly on the day of our date, but Martin showed up in jeans and a tank top. He immediately told me that his wife had no idea he was there, and then showed me her picture and told me her name. As I was digging into my Caesar salad, Martin told me that he liked to step on dead fish, using fish he bought at the supermarket. He would go home and do what I suppose you could describe as "tread fish." This practice didn't thrill his wife, who liked to eat fish, not stomp on them. Martin wasn't into eating fish at all, nor did he want to catch his own; too much bother.

For once in my life I was speechless, so it was a welcome diversion when my cell phone rang. It was Circuit City with an electronic message telling me when my new TV would be delivered, but I answered back with "What? Oh *no*. I'll come right away." I hung up and told Martin I had to go because my friend was sick. He fell for my story hook, line, and sinker. ❤

Quentin, 39
Accountant
SINGLE

Quentin left a very terse voicemail message, saying only that he was an accountant and had a full head of hair. Hard to imagine that would glean many callbacks for him. When I did call him back he was still a little uptight, but I put it down to his being busy. He chose a brasserie near his office for our lunch and was already at the table when I got there.

Clearly not a man with time to waste, Quentin got right down to business and asked if he could touch my lips. I demurred and asked why he would want to, anyway. This produced a veritable litany of lascivious lip worship. He told me he especially loved the cupid's bow of lips and proclaimed that he could lick Ally McBeal's lips all night long. Then he licked his top lip and let out a strained *ummmm* sound that I'm sure he thought was sexy. (It sounded more like constipation to me.) Quentin wanted me to go and put gloss on my lips, which he'd thoughtfully brought in case I didn't have any. Doodling lips on the napkins, he urged me again to gloss up my lips. I told Quentin he was making me feel very uncomfortable, to which he replied, "Good. When you're nervous, it makes the mouth twitch and the upper lip sweat, which is sexy." Will you be surprised, dear reader, to hear this guy got a big kiss-off? ❤

Morris, 40
Graphic Designer
MARRIED

Like dozens before and after him, Morris told me that he loved the way I spoke. I thanked him and tried to find out more about him, but Morris preferred to hear me speak. He asked me to say "water" over and over, as he found it sexy when I sounded the "T." After he had downed a few Scotches (with water, naturally), he asked me to say another word, one that starts with F and rhymes with "duck." It sounded so proper when an Englishwoman talked dirty, he said, it really turned him on. Would I please curse at him? He was such a creep that it was tempting, but I didn't want to give him the satisfaction. As he seemed to be partial to the letter T, I trilled a "Ta ta, toodle-oo" and took off. ❤

Ralph, 44
God Only Knows
SINGLE

Ralph was larger than life, almost cartoonlike. To say Ralph was big would be to say the Empire State Building is a bit tall. He was enormous—not fat, but just a huge man. He greeted me by kissing my hand and introducing me to the waitress, the barman, and a few other diners before ordering the waitress to "get Joseph out here." Joseph turned out to be the owner, and throughout our meal, Ralph beckoned a steady stream of employees and patrons to our table.

I didn't find out much about Ralph on our date, and when I asked what he did for a living, he replied, "I'm like an aspirin. I make headaches go away." And what do you do when the aspirin is giving you a headache? You thank him for meeting you, offer to pay for your share of the meal, and cringe when he orders everyone in the restaurant to come and say good-night to you. ❤

Pete, 48
Doctor
MARRIED

The first words of the message Pete left on my voicemail were "I'm a doctor, but I'm not wealthy." He then proceeded to drone on about his unhappy marriage and something about a government-imposed rule whereby he had to treat patients even if they only have fifty dollars to their name although his fee was four hundred dollars. Scintillating stuff. We arranged a lunch meeting for the following day and I noted that he didn't seem to have any difficulty getting away from his office. Perhaps that's why he wasn't prospering as a doctor.

Pete was about five feet nine and a little overweight. His dark hair was receding, but he wasn't bad looking. We shook hands and sat down to order some drinks, when out of the blue Pete asked if I had ever seen the movie *The Dentist*. I told him I hadn't, and he took great delight in telling me how the titular dentist would strap his female patients in the chair, legs akimbo, ply them with Novocain, then bite off their panties. As he told me this, he mimed the actions with relish, contorting his face as he made bite noises. I remained silent during this charming bit of thespian art, but I spoke up when he started in on a tale of a female patient of his. She had been depressed, he explained, but once he prescribed antidepressants she became the horniest woman in town. In fact it was so bad, she had taken to driving her car up and down a particularly bumpy street so she could orgasm. I told him I had to leave and he handed me his card with his name and all kinds of phone numbers on it, suggesting that if I wanted him after normal office hours, I should call the emergency line and they would contact him for me. As I left he pulled me close and tried to stick his tongue in my mouth. Gross and yuck! ❤

Gussy-Woo, 41
Internet Marketer
MARRIED

Don't be fooled by the silly name; this man was a liar of biblical proportions—and *he told* me so. Apparently he couldn't stop telling lies ... to everyone, for absolutely no reason whatsoever. I found it quite refreshing for a man to actually admit he was economical with the truth, as so many will have us believe their every spoken word is gospel. But Gussy-Woo admitted that he "just had" to lie and he enjoyed it, relished it even.

So what was with the name ...? That, it seems, was his wife's pet name for him and he wanted me to use it too. Nearly as icky was the way he peppered his conversation with a strange sound that can only be described as "*OOWEEE.*"

I asked him why he had answered my ad when he was a married man and he launched into his story. His wife was a "momma's girl" who cried at the drop of a hat. He had to pacify her over the slightest things or she would turn on the waterworks—*OOWEEE!*

Maybe I could have bought that, but he went on to inform me that his mother-in-law, Ann, owned a clothing store and she made him dress up in the ballgowns and dance with her while her husband, Bernard, was at work. He had done it a couple of times but he didn't want to do it anymore and he wanted my advice as to what he should do. *OOWEEE.* I asked if he had ever heard of the phrase "Just say no." Apparently, he hadn't, but more to the point, his mother-in-law knew that he was partial to a line or two of cocaine, and she was going to tell his wife if he didn't continue to be her dancing partner. He looked at me as if he was being offered his last meal before going to the electric chair, pleading with me to help him figure out what to do. Should he keep dancing with Ann to keep the peace or should he stand firm, say enough is enough, and break away? By now, *I* had had enough. I didn't care if Ann wanted him to samba the night away or bossa nova till daybreak. Gussy-Woo was on his own. *OOWEEEE!* ❤

Eric, 39
Mechanic
SINGLE

I want to warn you, dear readers, that this was a disgusting date. Eric had a vulgar fetish that he chose to share with me. Without delving too deeply into the realms of utter filth, can I just say that Eric liked to play with women's feces. Not their faces—you read it correctly, their feces!

As soon as he told me what he liked to do, I left. ❤

3

tops and bottoms

In hindsight it shouldn't have been surprising, but I was truly perplexed by the number of replies my tame little ad solicited from would-be slaves and masters. After dating one thousand men I can hardly claim to be an innocent, but time and again I was shocked to find that my perfectly bland-looking dinner companion honestly expected me to walk out of a restaurant with him and let him tie me up, teach me discipline, or worse. Others wanted to cast me in the dominant role. It's too, too strange to be sitting opposite a six-foot stranger when he tells you he wants only to worship and pamper you and will lick your kitchen floor clean if it pleases you! Another offered to wash all my dishes by hand, promising earnestly that my glassware will "sparkle like a new diamond." And of course there were a number who were seriously into pain.

It's really not that appealing to me when a man wants me to beat him, and if a boyfriend offered to beat me on the bottom with a rolled-up umbrella, it would be time for him to take a long walk off a short pier. Yet there was a certain fascination with these men, many of whom did not fit the stereotype I had had of submissive and dominant men. Quite a few of the submissive men told me that their stressful jobs and constant deadlines made them want to give up all control and be told what to do. (Memo to me: If I can't meet deadlines in future, should I race round to my editor and clean up her office?) But not all of them want to run through the house or office brandishing feather dusters and Pine-Sol. There's the submissive man who loves to be dominated only in a sexual way and wouldn't clean your house for twenty bucks an hour. He wants to be sat on, as in straddled. He may also like to be tied up, while the woman positions herself close to his mouth and, well, uses his tongue on her the way the slave man would use it on the kitchen floor! Another man I met just wanted to relinquish all control and be told exactly what to do. These men were completely open about their likes and wants. I'm still bemused at the thought of a man introducing himself to me, talking about his work at a major investment bank, and in the next breath asking if I would consider smacking his bottom until "the raised red welt marks look as though they are about to bleed."

The other side of the coin are those guys who want to be in total control, and while I listened in fascination, then boredom, to the dates who told me in no uncertain terms where and what they wanted to do to me, I was never afraid. After all, not too much can happen in a restraint, I mean restaurant, and I certainly never went anywhere else with them. There was much talk of being bound and gagged, sometimes with a Hermes scarf, darling, and at other times with a piece of twine from Home Depot. Of being shouted at and told what to wear and how to wear it, and in some cases being told what *not* to wear. Of each I would ask, "Excuse me, where's the turn-on for *me*?"—which generally got a blank stare in return.

They weren't all unlikable men. You may even find yourself

warming to a couple of them, and I don't just mean Alex, who liked to position his genitals very close to his coal fire and see how long it took for his "bits and pieces" to flambé! Each to his own, I guess. Just don't ask me to understand it and certainly don't expect me to join in. For my part, I have never known a man who could stack the dishwasher correctly, let alone produce sparkling silverware.

Steven, 40
Property Appraiser
SINGLE

Steven's message on my voicemail went on so long that he got cut off and had to call back to leave his phone number. He had told me how he looked, his height, and his weight. His favorite food was Chinese, he said, and he liked to drink Chardonnay. Also he was "extremely athletic" and "highly intelligent."

What Steven omitted from his biography was his penchant for dominant females. He saved this item until we were on dessert, at which point he mentioned that he'd like to "run something by me." I had no idea what it could be, and based on our prior conversation I wasn't expecting anything terribly strange.

"Once upon a time, there was a boy named Steven," he began. "Steven lived with his father and brother in a little town in Georgia. The father went off to work all day and the house was such a mess that one day Steven decided to have a real thorough spring-cleaning." I'll condense the story; when Steven told it, it took an hour. Apparently tidying up had turned him on and he had his first orgasm on a living room cushion, requiring more blissful cleaning up.

Ever since then, his most powerful and erotic orgasms came when he found a woman who would indulge his cleaning fetish. He liked to book a hotel room and send the woman there ahead of time to trash the place and then leave. Half an hour later Steven would come in, find the room in a mess, and begin to clean up. The woman would return to find the room a mess and chastise him verbally while he continued his work. The culmination of all this would be his orgasm, achieved only when he had completely restored the hotel room to its former glory.

Steven asked if I would enjoy something like that, and when I said no, he had the grace to admit it was a little "strange." He had been using the services of prostitutes for a while now, but he said he wanted to find a "real" woman who enjoyed it too. If it's the tidying he enjoys, maybe he should hire himself out as a maid—he'd have to keep his clothes on, but I can think of plenty of real women who'd love a clean house! ❤

Leon, 37
Architect
MARRIED

Leon and I met for dinner at The Four Seasons. He was a handsome, distinguished-looking man, quite tall and broad shouldered, and dressed in a dark blue suit. We had a wonderful dinner and good conversation, but when I asked why he was answering my ad when he was married, his reply surprised me. I was expecting the usual "my wife and I don't get along, and I want some new sex" routine, but Leon had a different song to sing. He and his wife had a decent marriage, no real problems at all. It was Leon's fetish that had caused him to respond.

Leon explained that he liked to have his bare bottom spanked. He liked it with an "open palm, a paddle, a shoe, or even a belt." Or he was happy to leave it to the spanker to come up with something more creative. He had met a couple of women in the last few months who had been happy to oblige. I was taken aback. He couldn't explain why he enjoyed a "good spanking," but he assured me that he derived intense pleasure from it. He liked to be able to feel the raised welts the following day. Of course, sitting down was difficult, but it was still overwhelmingly pleasurable.

His wife knew nothing of this practice, and he would never ask her to spank him. Had he never thought that if she *did* find out her husband was offering his bare bottom to strange women, she may well have wanted to spank him herself? ❤

Brian, 28
Picture Framer
SINGLE

I had to play Brian's message three times before I could understand what he was saying. I finally deciphered that he was "a little slave boy" and was hoping that I would discipline and toilet train him. I called him back and after a brief chat, we arranged to meet in a pizza place for lunch.

The minute I arrived, Brian asked what I wanted him to do, saying he had "references" to show me. I had to stop him from calling me "mistress." He was in full slave mode and raring to go! I was quite uncomfortable and told him to sit down and be quiet. I felt terrible, speaking sternly to him like that, but it seemed to be the only way to calm him down. I asked if he could be Brian the picture framer for a while, as I needed him to understand that I was not about to become his "mistress." I was also concerned that any time now, he was going to bring up the toilet training thing, and I was definitely *not* going there!

This was one occasion when spilling the beans had the opposite effect of what I intended. After I explained to Brian that I was doing research for a book and was not actually looking for a slave, he became even more excited. He wanted to help me, he said. He offered to type for me, or drive me to my dates. How about cleaning my apartment while I was out? Again, I told him no, but I let him know how grateful I was for the offer. Brian finally realized it was not to be and we said good-bye. As I caught a cab home to my messy apartment to type up my notes, I thought fleetingly of what might have been. . . . ❤

Quentin, 42
Management Consultant
SINGLE

Quentin and I met at a Chinese restaurant. We ordered, and while we were waiting for the first course, Quentin told me he was a fully trained slave. I've become an old hand at this confession thing, but I've still never come up with a fitting response to this particular declaration. All I could manage was "Oh, that's nice. How long have you been doing slave-work, then?" Whereupon Quentin launched into a tale that was only half as long as *War and Peace.* Sixteen years ago, it seems, he had a chance encounter with a dominatrix—and he had been hooked ever since.

He carried on with the sordid story, even when I told him it was becoming too graphic for me. He continued even as the waiter brought our food, and even as we began to eat. By now I really had had enough of Quentin. I told him to shut up and eat his dinner. He looked at me appreciatively, and in the meekest little voice you could imagine said, "Yes, Mistress." I started laughing, which finally did the trick; he didn't say another word until his cell phone rang. After asking my permission to answer it, Quentin spoke in his normal voice to a colleague about some work his company was doing for a well-known corporation. As if the situation were not already bizarre, when Quentin had opened his case to get the phone, a studded dog collar fell out. Two men at the next table had seen it and were clearly supressing their laughter.

When Quentin got off the phone, he became meek again

and wanted to play "slave and mistress." One of the guys at the other table pointed to the dog collar on the floor, saying, "Sir, I think something fell out of your case." Quentin thanked him, and without a hint of embarrassment returned it from whence it came. Soon thereafter, his mistress gathered her own things and left. ❤

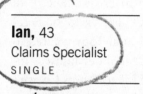

Ian, 43
Claims Specialist
SINGLE

Oh, Ian!

During our telephone conversation, Ian gave no indication of his painful passion; if he had, we would not have met.

But we did, and he was a nice-looking guy with sandy hair and a little mustache. He wore a suit, as he had just finished work, and I thought he looked quite fine. He ordered a bottle of wine for us and then asked me about myself. He'd been to London and was knowledgeable about the city. We had a decent chat for about twenty minutes, and then things took a turn for the ugly.

Ian was searching for a woman, he explained, who would enact a particular scenario he had in mind. She would wear white shoes with heels. While she was putting these on, Ian would remove all his clothes and lie face down on the carpet with his legs spread. White-shoe-woman would then tread on his penis and testicles until he cried.

Was that kind of thing appealing to me? he asked. Appalling is more like it, but I wanted to know why it was appealing to *him,* and wasn't it dangerous to have your privates trodden on by anyone, let alone a woman in heels? He agreed that it probably was dangerous, but that was the thrill—like kids jumping across train tracks when the train is coming.

Ian thanked me for meeting him and asked me not to think

badly of him. In truth, I felt a bit sorry. His idea of pleasure was absolutely alien to me and whenever I think about him, it makes me go queasy. Poor man, any way you slice it, he's downtrodden. ❤

Toby, 35
Loan Officer
SINGLE

"I am strong, physically and mentally, and I am in great shape. Call me. You won't be disappointed." When I did call him, Toby wanted to do all the talking, and told me a great deal about himself, including the fact that he was "dominant." I told him I wasn't submissive, and if he'd rather not meet, then that was fine. He still wanted to get together, so we arranged a date. After explaining in detail what he would be wearing, Toby finally said good-bye.

The day before our date, Toby called again and left me a message: "Do not wear pants if you are as petite as you said. Wear a short skirt." Needless to say, I wore a pantsuit!

As soon as I arrived, Toby announced, "I want to get this out of the way and then we can get on with our lunch."

Toby then asked me if I had ever experienced the "intensity that comes from being totally owned." No, I admitted, I hadn't. He went on to explain that "total ownership" had given him some of the best sex he had ever had. Before he could continue I told him that I had no interest in allowing another person to own me. The thought was completely abhorrent to me.

He brushed aside my comments and leaned very close to my face. Biting his bottom lip, he said, "You have been a bad girl. I need to punish you. You disobeyed Conran, didn't you?"

Conran? Who the hell is Conran?

As it turned out, when Toby was in dominant mode he called himself Conran. Even in full-on Master persona, he was more comical than menacing. He was still speaking through his bitten lip, and he looked like Popeye. I couldn't help it—I started to laugh.

Toby/Conran was patient. He waited for about three seconds before telling me that I was not supposed to find this funny. I explained to him that I couldn't, and wouldn't, be what this man Conran desired. He agreed that we were not a suitable "sexual" couple, but suggested that we could continue to meet platonically. It really wasn't worth getting into an argument with Toby, so I said I'd call him. Yes, I lied. Sorry and all that, but I didn't see an easier way out. Anyway, he's a loan officer. Surely he's become used to people being less than truthful. ❤

Paul, 53
Television Executive
SINGLE

I have put Paul in this chapter because he wanted to be compliant. However, he was only willing to give up control to a particular type of female.

Paul left a brief message mentioning that he was an executive for a major TV network. He said he would love to show me the sights of the city, and described himself as above average in every way. I called him, and we made a date for dinner.

When we met, Paul commented on how slim I was, but not in a complimentary way. His tone sounded more like disappointment. Once we were seated, he got down to business. The first words out of his mouth were "I don't think your thighs are large enough for what I need." (All those years of smothering my thighs with Dior Svelte have finally paid off, thank you, Lord.) I wasn't sure if we would be having dinner, as I was already out of favor. But Paul insisted we eat together, regardless.

Paul explained that he had a sexual turn-on that involved him (of course) and a slim woman with large thighs. This woman wraps her thighs around Paul, putting him into a headlock.

There they stay, locked together until she chooses to release him or he begs for freedom. Being pinned in this way made him feel powerless and totally carefree, he said. His erection is "hard as a rock," and the orgasm that follows is so fierce it leaves him drained.

Paul was very open about this specific desire and had no qualms telling me that I was not built for what he wanted. Somehow I managed to contain my disappointment, and on the way home, I realized Paul had given a whole new meaning to the term "thigh master." ❤

Scott, 50
Antiques Shop Owner
MARRIED

Scott and I had the briefest of dates. He was extremely rude, which was a complete shock because he had been very nice on the phone. When I arrived at the restaurant, he came over to greet me. He complimented me on my legs and we exchanged pleasantries. As soon as we sat down at a table, he leaned towards me and said, "If you've got a very hairy pussy, I will be your love fool." I said, "Stick with just being a fool, Scott." Then I was out of there. ❤

Roy, 33
Social Worker
SINGLE

Roy had a nice voice and left a very long message. He described himself as "cuter than could be" and assured me that he was my "man for all reasons and for all seasons."

When he turned up for our date, Roy was wearing a woman's coat, minus the belt. In the belt loops he had threaded three silky scarves woven into a braid. The coat didn't quite fit him, but he had tied the scarves around his stomach anyway, so there was a gap where the coat didn't close. A very strange look, indeed!

As it turns out, Roy was a slave in training. He had been training for six months and he felt he was ready to find a "mistress." I ordered a sandwich while Roy launched into all the chores and household tasks he would willingly perform for me, including licking my bathroom and kitchen floors clean. (That would be clean?) As a bonus, Roy would do all of his work in the nude and if I was satisfied with his services, I could loan him out to any of my female friends! He was, after all, the man for all reasons and seasons.

As nicely as I could, I declined his offer. Perhaps I was put off by the coat . . . ❤

Alex, 30
Photographer
SINGLE

Alex was a very busy man whose job took him all over the world. "Quite tall, above-average looks, and boyish charm" was his self-description. When we made a date for drinks at a hotel in the city, I recognized him immediately by the loads of camera equipment at his feet. After we shook hands and sat down, he showed me some photographs he had taken, and then he asked about me. He wanted to know where I lived in London. He had been there several times and named a few places that we both knew. All nice, normal stuff. Then Alex asked if he might share something with me. Some nachos, maybe? A dessert? No, neither of these things.

Alex wished to share with me the fact that he liked to toast his penis in the fireplace. He would stay there for as long as he could bear it. Of course he timed himself. Each time he did it, he would try to last a little longer. His penis was now a completely different color from when he first started this bizarre practice. He described how he would kneel into the fireplace and thrust his groin as close as possible to the flame. I didn't know what he expected me to say, so I just asked if it hurt. Of course it hurt; that's why he did it.

I asked why he had answered my little ad, which was unbelievably dull when compared to his penile roasting penchant. Alex suggested that I might like to watch. Why would he think that, I asked. Did my ad give off any "I would like to watch a man toast his private parts" vibes? No, he agreed it didn't; he knew it was a long shot. But he figured if you "don't strike a match, you'll never get a fire."

At the end of our date, I couldn't resist telling Alex that he really should be careful. "Yes, I know," he said, "my mother tells me that, too." His mother knows about this? That's the scariest part of all! ❤

Bill, 44
Fund Manager
SINGLE

Bill pleaded with me to meet him. He called five times, and one of those times he became the third caller, so I followed my rules. When I called him back, he thanked me over and over. We arranged a lunch meeting for the following day; I would know him by the yellow scarf.

I was a little bit late—only five or six minutes, but that was enough to worry Bill. He was pacing up and down outside the restaurant, yellow scarf in hand. Once he was reassured and we were seated, Bill told me he always took his scarf with him on blind dates. That way, it was easy for him to be identified. He went on to say that he had arranged more than twenty dates in the last few months, but only three women had turned up. (Personally, although I didn't say this to Bill, I think they *were* showing up. But when they saw Bill with his scarf, they decided to keep on walking.)

Suffice it to say, Bill was a very strange-looking man indeed. He wore his hair in a ponytail on top of his head, and he sported gloves with no fingers. To complete his look, Bill wore dark eye makeup, almost like Alice Cooper.

Over our lunch, Bill confided that he was in dire need of stern discipline, and he would welcome corporal punishment, bondage, or anything else I felt was necessary. With my recent experiences in the submissive world, I felt I could speak to Bill with some authority. I asked if it was his stressful job that made him want to surrender control over his sexual life.

At this he looked completely panic-stricken and said, "Why would you say that? You don't know where I work, do you? It's me, just me; the only way I can get an erection is when I am held captive. It has nothing to do with my job. I don't ever mix the two. Why would you say that? I don't want anyone at my job to know about this. That's why I answered the ad." He continued, "My job is a breeze. Most of the people there are assholes who don't know what day it is."

This date was not going well, so I told Bill I didn't want to discipline him, that it really wasn't my thing. I thanked him for the meeting and offered to get the check, to which he said okay and walked out the door. No good-bye, not even a handshake. Come to think of it, Bill, maybe a good smack would teach you some manners. ❤

Larry, 45
Salesman
MARRIED

I found it difficult to hear Larry's message because he delivered it in a low whisper. I later found out that he had been at home when he left the message. He had to speak softly so his wife wouldn't hear.

When I called him back, he seemed delighted and told me we would have a wonderful time together. Apparently we were going to "melt into erotic fantasy and yield to the power that is [pause] total compliance."

I told Larry straight out that we were going to a restaurant or a bar where we would have a quick drink and a chat. "No melting, no yielding, and no power! Got it? Good."

Far from being put off, Larry seemed to like my reaction. When we met, he told me that he loved to win a feisty female over. When he had her on her knees, bound, gagged, and handcuffed, he would just "take her." I asked why he didn't dominate his wife. The answer? Obvious. She didn't like it. In fact, she had hit him with a vase the first and only time he had asked if he could tie her up.

That had been eleven years ago and he had been fantasizing about meeting a compliant woman ever since. Though he wasn't dominant yet, he was certainly persistent.

When I asked why he thought I would be interested in his "melt, yield, power" games, Larry said that he didn't know, he just hoped.

As I left, Larry said, "Please, let's give it another try, *please*."

"No, Larry," I barked. "Good-bye." I walked out into the sunshine, wondering when the tables had been turned and I had become the mistress.

In all honesty, I don't think Larry's wife has anything to worry about. She knows how to control him, and as for his dominance over a compliant female—hand me a vase. ❤

non-starters

Of course I didn't need to lay eyes on some of my voicemail callers to know our relationship was not meant to be. More than one witty man was masturbating as he recorded his message. Some of them hung up when they reached the point of no return, but others actually left me their phone numbers.

Obviously I never returned calls from guys who were having "more than enough fun" with themselves. Nor did I return the calls from the guys serving time in jail. (Well, I couldn't actually return their calls anyway; most of them left a relative's phone number for me to make the initial contact.) And a note to any guys who might be answering a personal ad in the future: Know that there's never a good time to talk about rape. It's also not too clever to describe in detail your very favorite body part. Don't ask about mine either, for that matter. It's okay to ask me if I am slim, but it's not okay to say that you hope I'm not a big fat pig. You can ask if I am shapely, but it's not okay to suggest that you want to become acquainted with my breasts!

So, featured in this brief chapter are some guys who *really* said (or did) something so wrong that I didn't bother to meet them. Perhaps I missed out on something great. . . . You be the judge.

Tony, 38
Translator/Interpreter
SINGLE

It was around seven-thirty at night when I returned Tony's call. When I introduced myself, Tony said, "Ooh, I'm so glad you called. I'm just re-laxing at home with a glass of wine and my big, stiff cock." Excuse me?

I hung up. Despite two more calls from Tony, one apolo-gizing for his behavior, the other addressing me as "Ms. Attitude Problem," that introduction was the end of him. ❤

Bradley, 29
Roller-Blind Manufacturer
SINGLE

When I called Bradley back at 11 A.M. he claimed he was just wak-ing up. "I have that male morning tradition—I'm really hard. Can you help me?"

I hung up. I doubt that my response helped him much, but one never knows. ❤

Christopher, 44
Ceramics Company Owner
SINGLE

Christopher gave new meaning to the term "breast man." In his message he said, "I'd like to know how big the aureole of your breast is. I want to know if you can see it when you wear a bra. Does it show when you wear a bikini? Do you like it when men look at your breasts, and can you have an orgasm just by having your breasts touched?" He ended by saying, "I own a pottery business. I have money and I can buy you pretty bra ornaments. Call me!"

I doubt he would be eager to hear *what* I wanted to call him! ❤

Kenneth, 44
Driver
MARRIED

In Kenneth's message, he described himself as "hardworking and good-looking, with a fit body and broad shoulders."

During our phone chat, Kenneth told me that he didn't have a lot of money to spend. He wanted to meet me, but he couldn't afford to go out to a restaurant. Obviously, we couldn't go to his home (his wife wouldn't like it), so he asked if he could come to mine. When I told him that wasn't an option, he became angry and said, "Why, don't you trust me? I'm not going to rape you, you know."

Yes, I do know. Good-bye, Kenneth. ❤

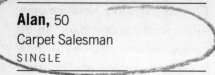

Alan, 50
Carpet Salesman
SINGLE

I laughed when Alan told me what he was wearing on the freezing cold evening when I called in response to the message he'd left: a pink ballerina tutu.

Why? It made him feel very horny, though he was at pains to assure me that he wasn't gay. He said that he'd found the outfit in a house his company recarpeted. The shoes didn't fit him, so he had to content himself with tiptoeing about and imagining himself onstage.

I pictured him in his outfit and decided not to take this any further. He accepted my decision but then asked, "Could you just come round and look at me, then? It turns me on." Sorry, Alan, it's no *pas de deux* for you. ❤

Martin, 40
Limo Driver
SINGLE

After telling me briefly about himself and his limousine company, Martin turned on the charm: "God, you sound so sexy. If you were here now I think I'd cream my pants!" Oops, the phone must have slipped out of my hand. Martin called the voicemail and asked if we had been cut off. Then he called again and asked if I had received his message. I ignored him. Guess he was having trouble getting *my* message! ❤

Chris, 47
Engraver
MARRIED

Chris mentioned that he was a married man, but said he hadn't had sex with his wife for seven years. "I really need sex badly," he moaned. "What do you say?"

I said, "I don't have sex badly," and moved on. ❤

John, 32
Insurance Agent
SINGLE

Dear John was six feet two. He had blue eyes and a full head of sandy blond hair. (So far, so good.) When I called him, he asked if I enjoyed large men. Here we go, I thought. John's cross to bear was a thirteen-inch penis (or so he said), and he carried on as though his endowment was a terrible ordeal. "No woman can take me—it hurts them all the time," he wailed. His ex-girlfriend had even left him for a man whose penis was quite small. (How, I wondered, does he know that?)

Before I could stop him, John repeated how large his penis was three more times. I told him we wouldn't be meeting and thanked him for calling. He asked if I had a friend he could meet, and if I did, would I please tell her about his penis? I assured him I would tell *everyone* about it. ❤

Barry, 41
Lawyer
SINGLE

Barry left an ordinary message, but when I called him back, he asked extremely personal questions: "What cup size are your tits?" I told him I wouldn't answer that. "Oh, then they're small, right? What about your ass, is it firm? I like women with nice tight butts." That was the end of Barry, no ifs, ands, and certainly no butts. ❤

Walt, 50
Engineer
SINGLE

Walt and I never spoke. His message was peppered with so many "ooohs" and "mmms" and "oh yeahs" that he left little doubt about what he was doing. When he was done, he had the nerve to leave his number and ask me to call him, telling me that he could do it "all over again" when we spoke. I hope he's holding his breath. ❤

Alex, 36
Gym Instructor
SINGLE

Alex began by describing himself in detail, giving all kinds of measurements, from pecs and abs to biceps and triceps. Then, in what he assumed was a sexy voice, he began to regale me with his sexual characteristics: "I am extremely oral, extremely well endowed, and extremely hard right now. I wish you were here," he continued. "I would grab you and pleasure you with my big rod."

Spare the rod, spoil the date, I always say. ❤

Curtis, 47
Paper Cup Company Owner
MARRIED

"Could you be my mommy on the phone?" Curtis asked when I called him back. Out of curiosity, I asked exactly what he had in mind, and he was only too happy to fill in the details. In his fantasy, he is six years old. He would like me to scold him and threaten to make him wear diapers if he "messes his pants" again. If I did this for him, he claimed, I would do wonders for his sexual potency. When he told me he had pooped in his pants while we had been talking, that was enough for me. I told him to stop talking shit and I hung up. ❤

Craig, 38
Broker
SINGLE

"Please come and see me," said Craig when I called him back after listening to his very ordinary message. I told him that I would be happy to meet him but not in his home, if that was what he was proposing.

"Oh, please do," he whined. "I'm harnessed and I'd love for you to see me."

At first I thought he had said "I'm harmless." But even then, I wouldn't have gone to his home. When I realized what he had actually said, there was no way I wanted to continue the conversation, let alone meet him. So I told him that I, too, was "tied up" and couldn't get together. Hey, Craig, hang in there. ♥

Neil, 37
Owner of Liquor Stores
SINGLE

All Neil wanted was for me to talk to him while he did "that jerky thing." More precisely, Neil requested that I repeat the phrase "sheer-to-waist panty hose" over and over again until he'd "arrived." Sorry, Neil, I've always been a thigh-high kind of gal, myself. ♥

Simon, 39
Artist
SINGLE

Simon was very articulate and told me a lot about himself. He was an artist, and asked if we could meet at his studio. I guessed that he wanted to get me there to do some kind of arty painting that would involve me taking off my clothes. I was wrong, but only sort of.

Simon said he wanted to play school, with me playing the part of the stern teacher and he the naughty student. He said he acted this scenario out with all the women he dated. (Did I mention that Teacher was to be naked?) He always ended up getting spanked by the teacher, after which she (I) would give him homework.

I gave this proposal a flunking grade. ❤

Lou, 45
Hotel Reservations Clerk
MARRIED

This is the exact message that Lou left on my voicemail: "Hello, my name is Lou, short for Louis. My phone number is 555-7576. I like to have a woman watching me while I urinate. Would this interest you? Sorry if you don't like this. If I don't hear from you, then could you ask any of your girlfriends if they might like it? Thank you in advance."

No, no, thank *you!* ❤

Trey, 40
Head of a Video Production Company
SINGLE

Trey's extremely detailed message gave his height, weight, and almost all his body measurements, including his chest, neck, and shoe sizes. Perhaps he thought he'd dialed the suit department at Macy's! No, it seems that Trey was just very thorough.

When I called him back, he wanted to know all my sizes, too, but seemed to be especially concerned with my hair. Trey was eager to know its color, style, and texture, and asked, "What, precisely, is the style of your hair right at this moment?" To be honest, the "style" could only be described as that fashionable "dragged through a hedge" look, but of course I didn't say that to Mr. Picky-Wicky. For his benefit, I told him that I had wavy auburn hair that fell past my shoulders. This wasn't enough for Trey. "What texture is it?" he wailed. "Why aren't you blond?" Then he said decisively, "Send me an e-mail with a picture of your hair, and if I like it I'll meet you." When I refused, he let rip with a mouthful of abuse, calling me and most of the women of America "fucking bitches!"

Trey soon called back and left a message saying he was very sorry, and that he'd been under a lot of stress. Would I please give him another chance? And had I ever *considered* going blond? ❤

5

eat, drink, and be foolish

You do the math: One thousand dates means one thousand drinks and/or meals. That's a lot of Chardonnay under the bridge and more than a few miles of pasta primavera. So you can excuse me for being fed up to here with food. That wasn't, however, what was up with these men, all of whom had some kind of food fixation—many of which I had a chance to observe during the course of our meeting. Most of them were just plain odd, but there were a couple that used food for their sexual gratification. Before your imagination runs away, rest assured that the stories that follow are pretty mild—no X-rated stuff here. Let's just say they liked to do things with their food other than eat it.

Personally, I don't like any food enough to get my knickers in a twist about it, but for these guys food clearly played a major role in their life dramas, and there were enough of them that they merited a chapter of their very own. These weren't the worst dates I had, but as for seeing any of them again . . . sorry, I've had enough.

Ian, 33
Construction Worker
MARRIED

Ian gave an accurate description of himself as "just average everything." He wasn't unpleasant, but he seemed to have been honest.

When I arrived at our meeting place, I was surprised to see that it looked like a grocery store. Then I realized that towards the back there was a cafeteria. Ian was waiting for me with two empty plastic containers. Apparently, we had to go to the food counter, select the items we wanted, and then weigh them. He asked that I try to keep my selections below one pound; he didn't want to spend a lot of money on me until he knew if he liked me. With a gracious smile, I piled my container as high as I could.

Ian looked as if he were about to cry. "No, no, I told you, you've got too much. Now you can't put it back—they won't let you." When I told him that I would be more than happy to pay for my own food, he calmed down.

When we found seats, Ian quickly polished off his meal and began to help himself from my container. I asked him to stop, but he said he had never tried many of the items I had chosen, so I should share.

By this point, I was sick of him. He was cheap, cheating on his wife, and, in his own words, he was just average. I closed my carton and told him I was leaving and taking my food with me. As I neared the door, he called out that with my attitude I would never meet anyone. Well, at least I wouldn't starve. ❤

Shawn sounded pretty normal on the phone. He was cheerful and nice and asked if we could meet up for breakfast, as he worked all day and sometimes at night. I agreed, and we decided on a diner we both knew. He described himself as being of "average height and looks, but a very sincere man."

When I arrived, Shawn was waiting and stood up at the table, waving the menu. As I approached him, he smiled and put the menu on his head, balancing it until it fell off. He was laughing at this trick and obviously having a wonderful time.

What was I getting into? I wanted to run away. Instead, I sat down and ordered coffee and toast; it appeared that Shawn had already placed his order. He just kept on smiling, not saying a word to me. I didn't say anything either, and the situation was too strange for words. But it got worse.

When the waitress brought our food, Shawn examined his fried eggs with great interest. He actually spoke to me then, saying, "I have to eat all the white first without breaking the yolk, or else." Or else what?

It was a sight to see, this grown man delicately cutting around the egg yolk so as not to break it. He was successful with the first one, but then he broke the second. Oh no!

Shawn started to become very distressed, and ordered another two eggs. Apparently he couldn't go to work until he ate two egg whites without breaking the yolks.

I was really getting into this, willing him on. I remembered playing a similar game with a candy that you had to suck without crunching, so I knew the agony he was going through. Mind you, I was ten years old when I'd played that game.

Eventually Shawn did it, so all was well. By this point it was time for him to go to work at the traffic school, and I was worn out. So much excitement, and all before 10:00 A.M.! ❤

Patrick's message was quite abrupt, and had he not been caller number three, I would have happily deleted him. However, we chatted briefly and arranged a date for lunch. We arrived at the restaurant at the same time, and I recognized him by the red bow tie he'd said he would be wearing. Still quite brusque, he said, "We'll order our food, and then we'll talk."

Patrick ordered a steak, but he needed to know what kind of fries they had. On learning they were large "steak fries," he looked happy for the first time since we'd met. I ordered the pasta. Hearing this, Patrick clasped his hands together with his elbows on the table and asked earnestly, "What do you like to do with food other than eat it?" I wasn't ready for this and couldn't think of anything smart to say. He went on, "I'm surprised you ordered pasta. What can you make with that?" I agreed that I probably couldn't "make" anything with it.

When the food arrived, Patrick took his fries and began to build. He laid two fries one way, then another two the other way on top, and so on until he had a tall stack that he announced with pride was a parking lot. He then carefully ate the top floor of the parking lot, all the while warning the cars parked there that the lot was dangerous and they needed to be removed immediately!

I ate my food in silence. I learned nothing about Patrick other than what I observed. When he had eaten all his fries, he ordered some more and started again. By then I had finished my food and was bored with all this construction, so I excused myself and offered to pay the bill. He refused, saying that he was meeting someone else after me, and anyway, he wanted me to go, since I was no fun and didn't know how to play. "Would you please leave?" he said. "Can't you see I'm working?"

By now he had stacked the second helping of fries, and as I

left, I took some childish pleasure in bumping the table so that they all fell down. ❤

"I want to take you to a little diner where they serve real mashed potatoes," Michael told me when we made our initial contact. I mustered up as much enthusiasm for potatoes as I could and agreed to a meeting the following evening.

He was there when I arrived, and told me that he had been "concerned" that I would not show up. It wasn't long into the date before I was wishing that I hadn't.

Before we'd even ordered, Michael got a few things off his chest.

He wanted me to know that he lived in a trailer, but that he was nothing like the people I knew who lived in trailers. I told him I didn't know anyone who lived in a trailer, and asked why he thought I would care.

He replied that he was "concerned" that when (not if) I went to his home, I would take a dim view of the entrance to his park and therefore get the wrong impression of him as a person.

When I assured him that I would never be so shallow, he ordered my food (without asking what I wanted) and told the server to bring three orders of mashed potatoes. Clearly he looked forward to his favorite dish.

Our meal arrived and one mouthful of "real mashed potatoes" told me they weren't! As the meat on my plate was also only masquerading as steak, I didn't see any point in making a fuss. I picked at my food as Michael went on to inform me that he didn't have a washing machine. He didn't find it too much of a bother, though, as even here in Florida's hot climate he didn't sweat too much. He could wear a shirt three and sometimes four times before he had to wash it. Michael then launched, apparently without irony, into the difficulties he had meeting the opposite sex. I'd had enough, but when I suggested that we call it a night, Michael said he was "concerned" that I hadn't eaten enough and asked the waitress for a container to put my food in so I could "eat later and think of him."

He asked if I wanted to go to his place and watch TV, and when I said no, he asked if I wanted to see him again.

As nicely as I could, I told him that I didn't think we had much in common, but that it had been very nice to meet him. Michael spat back, "I don't want to see you again, either. You're just the same as the others, but you're worse. You think you're special because you're from England, but you're not." And then he left, taking my leftovers with him. ❤

Allen, 33
Teacher
MARRIED

Have you ever laughed so hard you got a pain in your side, and even then you couldn't stop laughing so the pain went on and on? That just about describes my date with Allen. He was a nice-looking man with blond hair that he wore in a ponytail. We met for a drink, and as he gulped down his whiskey, he looked at me and said, "I can't have an orgasm unless I have maple syrup on my member. Is that all right?" He was looking at me very intensely, awaiting my reply. All I could think to say was "All right for what?"

Allen told me that he'd discovered the joys of having a "sticky dick" at the tender age of sixteen and that the feeling of a gooey substance (with or without a partner) had now become a necessity. By now we were both laughing, and Allen confessed that he felt like an idiot. I did try to be serious, but it just wouldn't happen. Finally, he shrugged and said cheerfully, "I guess if we tried to have sex together we'd just end up laughing, right?" I agreed, and made no jokes about being "stuck" on him or what a "sweetie" he was, although I did say that he should "stick" with his wife. ❤

Phil, 40
Management Consultant
SINGLE

Phil loved Lyonnaise potatoes. When we met, he told me that he knew all about this famed French dish and was looking for a mate who would share his enthusiasm. Over the course of our date, I found out next to nothing about Phil except for this obsession. "Most American women don't know about Lyonnaise potatoes," he told me sadly, shaking his head. I knew little of the dish except that I enjoyed it, so I had to bow to his superior culinary knowledge. Of course Phil had chosen a venue based on its potato potential, and his sense of anticipation was palpable. Then tragedy struck.

When the long-awaited Lyonnaise dish arrived, it wasn't authentic. We were served a few potatoes in a pretty casserole with a scattering of baked onions on top.

Phil could hardly speak, he was so incensed! He summoned the manager to point out the kitchen's failure and was told, "This is the way we serve them here. If you don't like it, tough!"

I really couldn't find it in my heart to get passionate about the potatoes, but I did think it was rude of the manager to speak that way to Phil. Phil clearly wasn't about to let it slide, and was on his feet now and ready to "take it outside." When he wouldn't calm down, I told Phil I was leaving. He kissed my cheek distractedly and told me he'd call later; he had to get this sorted out first! ❤

Graham wanted to meet with me on Friday evening, as he had tickets for a "cruise to nowhere." Sensing my hesitation, he quickly assured me it was only for four hours and that we could have fun and gamble too. What the heck, I figured, wasn't I taking a gamble every time I embarked on a new date?

He told me he would be dressed "all in black; women like that," and we arranged to meet at the reception area. True to his word, he was clad in black from head to toe and clutching a copy of the paper that had run my ad. He greeted me warmly, saying, "I like your outfit; do you like mine?" Before I could answer, he steered me over to the reception desk, where he complained about having to pay twenty dollars for each ticket; since his brother owned three restaurants in the area and was always sending people on the cruise Graham felt that our tickets should be "comped." He made a big show of putting money down on the counter, all the while shaking his head in disbelief. As he continued to express his disgust, the receptionist gently told him that the tickets *were* free; in fact, *everybody*'s ticket was free; it was a free cruise. They made their money from gamblers. Graham looked suitably sheepish and said, "Oh, what am I talking about, then?"

By now there was a huge line behind us and I just wanted to get on the ship. Constant announcements over the loudspeaker informed us of various other activities on board; one of them was a hot-dog concession on deck three, where for $2.50 you could buy a "foot-long dog." Graham said we should check out the free buffet, which was "kind of basic, but what do you expect for nothing, shrimp and lobster?" Apparently Graham did, for he complained to me that he couldn't eat that garbage and he dragged me off to deck three for a hot dog. When we found the stand Graham was appalled to find that there was no one there to sell us the foot-long delicacy that he so desired. After waiting for maybe two or three minutes he said he'd had enough, went behind the counter, and served himself. Instantly, four security men had surrounded Graham, with one yelling, "Drop the hot dog, fella, put the hot dog down . . . now." But Graham yelled back, saying that he wasn't going to steal the hot dog, he would have left the money on the side. Then he told them they were jerks and had been watching too much TV, adding, "What did I do, grand theft wiener?" As he attempted to take a bite, one of the security guards snatched it away and told him he was going to arrest him, to which Graham told him he had no jurisdiction and anyway they were a bunch of cocksuckers. That didn't go down too well, for Graham was handcuffed and marched off to a holding cell, where I was informed he would be kept until we returned to United States soil and he could be "turned over to the authorities." With that, he was gone and I was left standing there. I couldn't go home; I had another two hours of this cruise to nowhere to get through. I never did see Graham again and have no idea what happened over the 12-inch crime he'd committed. ❤

Howard, 44
Engineer
SINGLE

When Howard and I had our telephone conversation, he came across as quite normal. He asked just one strange question. Though lots of men wanted to know what type of woman I was and what type of men I preferred, Howard was the first to ask what blood type I had. I wondered why he would want that information, and he replied that he needed to know so that he could order the correct food for my blood type. When I asked why he had answered my ad, he replied, "It's in my blood."

Too many people that he knew were putting the wrong foods into their bodies and causing themselves damage, he explained. Furthermore, I shouldn't eat too much red meat and definitely no tomatoes. There was to be no shrimp for me and I could have only one egg per week!

Now, I don't portray myself as the fittest female that ever lived, but I am not heavy and I don't smoke, neither of which could be said for my date. Health-conscious Howard was at least thirty pounds overweight, and if he was so concerned about my health, I don't know what he was doing blowing his cigarette fumes my way. Surely a cigarette is far worse for the body than shrimp cocktail or a three-egg omelet!

I gently suggested his priorities were a tad askew, but he brushed it off and instead asked, "Is your second toe longer than your big toe?" Why? Because if it were, then the chances were quite high that I could be a lesbian! I assured him that I was heterosexual, but that wasn't enough. He demanded to see my toes, right there in the restaurant. When I refused, he told me that I was so "petulant" because of the food I ate. (Here we go with the food again.) Through a cloud of cigarette smoke he offered to make out a food plan for me, and promised that it would make me a better person all around. He also suggested that I eat more bananas to improve my disposition.

As far as I was concerned, this guy *was* bananas! With all Howard's talk about the foods I should and shouldn't eat, I hadn't actually gotten around to eating anything on our date. When I left Howard at the table, puffing away, I marched out onto the street and bought a hot dog with onions and ketchup. Here's to your health, Howard! ❤

6

show me the money

Who says money isn't everything? Seems like it's always the highly paid actor, mogul, or supermodel making that statement, never the guy working two jobs with three kids to support. Given my choice I'd rather have some than not. But you know what? Money really *isn't* everything, at least if these men are anything to go by. They certainly make a strong argument for the saying that money can't buy happiness. Money also can't buy love, and it doesn't make you a nicer person.

The men in this chapter had money, and plenty of it—and they wanted me to know it. (Either that, or the pursuit of wealth had left them with nothing much else to speak about.) Some were clearly relative newcomers to the world of big bucks—hardly "to the manner born." They could afford an upscale residence and car, and their money could get them into any place they desired, but they had not acquired the social graces to go along with these posh accoutrements. But these men knew the power money has, especially where romance is concerned. (How many indigent seventy-five-year-olds have you seen with buxom young blondes on their arms?) They simply assumed that talking about what kind of cars they drove, how many homes they had, and their amazing financial acumen made them a catch in any woman's eyes. Suffice it to say that money doesn't make you smart, either.

Joseph, 60
Retired
MARRIED

Joseph said on the phone that he loved the "sound of me" and wanted to take me to dinner, even if I "looked like the back end of a bus!"

"Your voice is so sweet," he said generously. "If you're a dog, I'll close my eyes and listen to you talk." What a charming date this was going to be!

Joseph chose the venue for our meeting, and it was very busy and extremely upmarket. I was shown to the table, where a Tony Curtis look-alike awaited me. "Ah, you're gorgeous," he told me. "You shouldn't put yourself down!"

I was confused. *He* had been the one with concerns about my appearance. Bloody cheek of the man!

Joseph ordered Champagne and sat back in his chair. Clasping his hands together at the back of his head, he said, "Tell me all about you." I told Joseph what I wanted him to know and then I asked about him. After twenty-five minutes of jabber, all I found out from Joseph was that he was rich. Very, very rich.

He asked if I knew that money was the most important thing in the world, that without it a person amounts to nothing. He went on and on about his apartment here and his condo there and all his worldly goods. It was boring. *He* was boring.

But the restaurant was delightful. There were celebrities at a nearby table, and if Joseph had just stopped bragging about his possessions for a while, it would have been rather a pleasant date. Alas, he just couldn't stop, and even the stars weren't enough to keep me there. ♥

Owen, 67
Retired
MARRIED

"I saw yer ad and yer a sexy soundin' woman. I'd like ta take ya ferra dinna, waddya say?" Owen sounded like a mobster, or at least like the mobsters I had seen in the movies. (I'm from London—what do I know about the Mob? Though I do suppose they don't usually have names like Owen!) I was looking forward to meeting him. When we did meet, he turned out to be a tall, gray-haired man, dressed in a suit. He greeted me with a kiss on each cheek, addressing me as "doll."

When we were seated, Owen said, "So lookatchoo, all the way from London. What time is it there, ten hours behind America?" I told him we were actually five hours ahead. But he wasn't listening; he was already regaling me with tales of a visit he'd once made to England. In fact, most of our conversation focused on Owen and his wayward ways.

The bottom line was that Owen had plenty of money, so he never went with hookers! He'd been married "forever" but liked to spend his money on other women. "Real" women. That's why he had answered my ad. He answered ads "all the freaking time" but apparently most of the women lied about their freaking size.

Owen asked how long I would be in town and offered to take me "anywhere you wanna go, doll." When I made my excuses, he didn't want me to go and said, "Come on, you just got here, have another drink, or a cuppa cwoorfee, and let's bull-shit a little." So I ordered a cwoorfee and we did just that, I guess. When I finally left him, Owen said he would leave it up to me to get in touch, but he hoped that I would. "Me an' you," he said, "I could show you some places in this city that most people don't even know exist, places that don't even open 'til two in the mornin'. Bye, doll, cwoorl me."

He wasn't really a bad guy, Owen, just not my cup of cwoorfee. ❤

Clement, 56
Import/Export Businessman
SINGLE

Clement's message promised me dinner at his favorite restaurant, where as his guest I could order anything at all. It was a very expensive restaurant, but he assured me he could afford it. You can imagine how impressed I was.

I was, however, impressed by his honesty. Clement had described himself as ugly, overweight (no, he said, change that to very heavy), and loud. Sure enough, he was telling the truth. I spotted him easily at the appointed restaurant, and as I sat down, he asked if I would care for some Champagne. I told him that would be lovely. "Lovely, lovely," he repeated loudly, in a mocking tone.

When my food arrived, Clement repeatedly asked me if it was okay. If it wasn't, he announced, he would "go over someone's head." I assured him everything was fine, hoping to placate him. He really *was* loud, and he sounded angry even when he was just ordering bread. I found myself speaking extra-quietly, hoping he would tone it down a little, but he didn't take the hint. Or perhaps he did but just didn't care what I, or anyone else, thought.

As we ate, Clement said, "Look at me, one ugly s.o.b., but I got money, and money speaks all languages, so what do I care? I never eat dinner alone, but I would without a fat bank balance." Louder now, he continued, "Think only a mother could love a face like this? Nah, I got women comin' out my ass."

I didn't really want to be one of those women, thank you very much. As it was getting late, I told Clement I should be getting home. He asked me to stay until we both got "bombed," suggesting that maybe I would find him attractive with a few more drinks in me! Clement, they haven't made a whiskey strong enough. ❤

Jon, 36
Caterer
SINGLE

"Shall I pick you up in my Porsche?" was the first question Jon asked during our phone conversation. He went on to tell me all about the car's special engine, the spoiler he'd put on it, and even the price. Mr. Moneybags said that he was not the kind of guy you'd find typically answering ads, and he was eager to let me know just what a catch he was. We arranged a date, and Jon told me that I would know him because he would be sitting outside the restaurant, on the hood of said Porsche.

Luckily it was raining that night, and although I did see the car parked in front, there was no Jon perched atop. He had decided to wait inside, and when I walked through the door, he appeared out of nowhere, looking very flustered. He had one hand on his hip and the other held out to the side, in a pose that gave the impression that he was about to burst into "I'm a Little Teapot."

The reason for his frustration was the seating arrangement. Jon had apparently specified a particular table, which he had learned now wasn't available. Jon was not a happy teapot. I told him not to worry, that we could just sit at the table that was available, but Jon wouldn't hear of it.

"Do you know who I am?" he bellowed. "Do you know how much money I spend here?" They obviously didn't, nor did they seem to care.

Eventually the manager came over and asked Jon to lower his voice or he would have to leave. At that, Jon lost it completely. His voice rose several octaves as he berated the manager, hurling insults.

Throughout this whole saga, he didn't remove his hand from his hip, though the free hand made several obscene gestures. As I stood to the side, fascinated by the scenario, Jon began kicking the manager! Yes, kicking.

No one said a word to me as I opened the door and stepped into a waiting taxi. I never heard a word from Jon, so I have no idea what the culmination of the evening's events was. However, when I was going past the restaurant a few days later, I noticed that the front window was being replaced. ❤

Ben, 75
Widower
RETIRED

Ben was a little silver-haired man, originally from New Jersey, who told me he'd come to Miami to die. He looked so fragile when we met that I was only hoping he didn't pop off on our date. He wanted me to understand that he had plenty of money; in fact, he was part of a consortium of men who gambled every afternoon, all of them high rollers. According to Ben, the four of them were worth well over fifty million dollars.

He was dressed in light blue polyester trousers with a light blue short-sleeved shirt and white shoes and socks—Miami's uniform for the older man. At his suggestion, we met at a restaurant for an early bird dinner. (I have since heard the joke that the "early bird" is the state bird of Florida.) It was only 5:30, but you had to be seated before 6:00 P.M. to get the discount. When I ordered wine, he told me that it wasn't included in the deal, and I should have tea or coffee instead, but I told him it was okay and that I'd pay the extra, which seemed to mollify him. As Ben took a trip to the salad bar, I looked around and saw that I was the only person in the restaurant under age seventy. Oh well, I figured, at least I was safe with this crowd.

After polishing off his food, Ben leaned across to me and asked if I was looking for "a little action in the sex department." I told him I wasn't, but thanked him for the offer. He looked disappointed and called for the bill, asking me, "Do you want me to pay for you? I will, you know." I told him that wasn't necessary, and that I'd even pay for him, too. Including the tip, the bill for our three-course meal was only twelve dollars. It was only ten past six, but I guess action man had to get home.

As we walked to the parking lot, I couldn't help noticing that almost all the cars were parked erratically. It looked as though the drivers had just driven in, turned off the ignition, and walked away. Ben had practically parked his car sideways, spanning three spaces! As I watched Ben drive off, I could hardly see his head. God knows how he saw over the steering wheel! With his hazard lights flashing away, he tooted his horn and waved good-bye to me as he sailed onto the open road. ❤

7

married men

For all my worldly ways and my considerable experience with the personals, I was appalled by the sheer numbers of married men who are out there dating. (I'm sure you've noticed that there are married men in all the other chapters as well; if I had put every married man I met here, it would be half the book!) Of course they used all kinds of ridiculous euphemisms to avoid admitting their marital state. There's "I'm attached," "I'm kind of married," "I'm sort of with someone right now," and my personal favorite, "I'm married in name only." To these men I would like to point out that Siamese twins are *attached*; *you* are *married*.

Then, of course, there are the little darlings who run around pretending they are single while "wining, dining, and if they had their way sixty-nine-ing" women from the personals. Come on, guys, it's not as if it "just happened" if you buy the paper, read the personals, find one you like, and call up and leave your number.

What was especially appalling was how many married men gave me very personal information about themselves and their families. I don't mean just home telephone numbers, although that was stupid enough, but on more than one occasion I saw photographs of the smiling couple with their kids. I was given business cards from their companies and asked to be discreet when I called. I assured them I would, and they trusted me completely. They were right to, for I have no wish to break up anyone's marriage, but the next woman they meet may not feel the same way.

After a few dates with married men, I began to calculate how far into the date it would be before he felt comfortable (or foolhardy) enough to tell me he was not the singleton he had pretended to be. Would he confess before the appetizer, or would I have to wait until the check arrived? Their stories, I'm afraid, were numbingly similar: The wife had let herself go, didn't want sex (or at least not the kind *he* wanted), or worked too much or not enough. He stayed with her only for the kids/dog/house/finances. All I can say is, lucky women to be married to such thoughtful blokes.

To the married men of America I say, I don't care if your wife got fat, doesn't understand you, or devotes too much time to her job, kids, cats, etc. If you're not happy, leave! Part company before you start cheating on her, and then there may be a little respect left between you.

Oliver, 40
Pharmacist
MARRIED

Sometimes I'm just astonished at how little men understand what women want. Over drinks, Oliver told me that his wife had "let herself go," a cardinal sin, and that they no longer got along because of it. He'd been very particular about my appearance when we arranged to meet, demanding to know my exact height and weight. Apparently I passed muster.

In addition to gaining weight, Oliver's wife had quit doing household chores. Because of this, he said, no one came to their house anymore. He admitted that his wife traveled quite a bit for her business, but he didn't see that as a valid excuse. As he talked, I figured Oliver was just another guy looking for an unpaid counselor. But I was wrong; he wanted me to be his unpaid cleaner, with a slight difference.

In a nutshell, this was his idea: I would go to Oliver's home while his wife was away. Once there, I would dress up in a maid's outfit and clean his house! I would be wearing an outfit that was short, very short. My nipples would be on show and I would wear no knickers. Oliver would be so turned on by the "clean and tidy house" (not the cleaner, mind you) that he would want to have sex with me. When I had finished cleaning, that's what we would do.

Did this guy know anything at all about women? I told Oliver that I didn't like to do my own housework, much less that of a stranger. As for having sex with him, I'd rather clean my oven! ❤

Davey, 40
Musician
MARRIED

This was one of my few small-town dating experiences, and it was a strange one. Davey was in a jazz combo that was the house band at a popular local venue, which happened to be the only nightclub in town. At his suggestion, we met there for drinks.

Most of the patrons wore jeans, and I felt a little overdressed. It seemed as if all five hundred forty residents of the town were in the club, which was packed. I peered through the crowd, wondering how I would find Davey, and finally asked a waiter to help.

"Would you be Mish-ale?" he asked. Close enough, I figured, and replied in the affirmative. The waiter then picked me up and swung me around saying, "I'm Davey!"

I wasn't sure what was going on here. Was the waiter also a musician? It seemed that was it, and in fact the bouncer was the combo's drummer. Davey raced off to get me a drink and then pulled me along to a table near the stage with a "reserved for stars' guests" sign written in blue marker. All the while, he was calling out greetings: "Hey Jacky! Yo Chucky! What's going on, Billy?" Everyone in the whole town had a name that ended in the letter "Y." Davey apologized that he had to rush off for a little while, leaving me at the table while he took drink orders.

As I sat there people-watching, I began to wonder why Davey had asked me here. He was a married man, after all, in a town where it seemed that no one was a stranger. It was all very bizarre! The next time I saw him, Davey was on stage, doing his musician thing. He dedicated a song to me, and two songs later, he sent one for "my darlin' spouse, who yesterday had muh baby." Everybody clapped and whistled as Davey belted out his rendition of the Billy Joel classic "I Love You Just the Way You Are."

I was beginning to feel very uncomfortable and decided that it was now time to make my getaway. When I got up, though, Davey stopped singing and called out, "Wassup Mish-ale?" I was on my feet by now and wasn't prepared to be seated again, so I told Davey, and the entire club, that I needed to go to the ladies' room. How embarrassing! Obviously I went to the exit instead.

On my way out of town (after passing the "PLEASE DRIVE CAREFULLY, WE CARE ABOUT Y'ALL" sign at the town limits), I stopped at a drive-through for a cheeseburger. The server asked where I was from, and when I said London, he came out to look at me. I glanced at the tag pinned to his uniform, and sure enough, his name ended in Y. ❤

Robert Joseph (Ladies Love), 49
Pastor
MARRIED

"Hello, my angel. I love that voice of yours. Whatever you do today, call me. And remember, God loves you."

This opening didn't fill me with pleasant anticipation, but he was my third caller and I was determined to stick to the rules. Robert Joseph said he was "overjoyed and bursting with privilege" that I had "ordained" to call him, but then he knew that I would, as God had said so. (Huh? Did God also know he was my third caller?)

For our date, he chose a down-home, "cooking like your momma makes" diner. I was anticipating a touchy-feely, you've seen 'em on TV–type preacher, and that was exactly what Robert Joseph delivered. I held out my hand as a means of introduction and was met with, "Oh no, darlin'! You come closer and let us really know you." Us? He was certainly big enough to be two people. Robert Joseph moved in, and pudgy arms and an overpowering waft of cologne engulfed me. He kissed the top of my head and said, "Mmmm, you smell *sooo* good."

Taking my hand, he led me to a table where a carafe of red wine awaited us. He continued to hold on, even as we sat down. I asked him to pour me a glass in the hope that he would relinquish my hand, and at last he let go and asked me how I was feeling. I answered, "I'm fine," and Robert Joseph said strongly, "No. How are you *really* feeling?"

"Uh, still fine," I replied. There was a long silence until at last he solemnly told me, "I believe in God and conscience." I told him I thought that was good, and then Robert Joseph asked me, "What do you want? What do you really want?" He sounded like the Spice Girls!

By then, my fondest desire was to be somewhere far away from pastor Robert Joseph. Instead, I asked for a cup of coffee and a chicken sandwich. I knew this was not what he wanted to hear. He pulled from his pocket a bottle of Stetson cologne and a little maroon diary with the name of his church stenciled on the front in gold lettering. After passing the diary to me, another hand-holding episode ensued. Then Robert Joseph dabbed his forehead with a napkin he had just doused with Stetson, winking at me and saying, "Ladies love Stetson."

I excused myself for a moment, and when I returned, the pastor said, "Let's get down to business. I am married but I am also a man. I have really known some wonderful women from personal ads. See, God is a man too, so it's not a problem. Allow yourself to believe."

I believed all right. I believed I was sitting with a cheating, fornicating, hypocritical wolf in sheep's clothing, and I told him so. Then I got up and left, unconsciously clutching the diary. When I got home, I leafed through my souvenir and found that Robert Joseph had marked the dates he would be free for a liaison. It crossed my mind to send it back to the church, but I decided against it. One meeting with Robert Joseph was quite enough, and if I never smell Stetson again, it will be just fine with me. ❤

Bob, 42
Teacher
MARRIED

Bob was such a know-it-all, even for a teacher. He had been to London twice, so of course he was an expert on my hometown. He also turned out to be an authority on infidelity. His wife was anorexic, according to him, but that was fine, as far as he was concerned—she could do whatever it took to stay slim. He hated fat women.

Bob himself was no oil painting, let me tell you. He was around five feet nine with a skinny frame and gray hair that he swept to the side. His wife knew he cheated on her, he claimed; it was "part of life." He and his wife had been married for fourteen years, and he told me that no man could be with just one woman for that length of time.

The conversation moved to the linguistic differences between England and America. At first it was lighthearted—for instance, if a British guy says, "Hi, I'm Randy," he's telling you he's horny, and if I were to ask a man to "knock me up in the morning," I'm only asking for a wake-up call, not for him to be the father of my child. So far, so good. Then Bob asked why English men call women Sheilas. I replied that that's actually an Australian term; English men may use the word "bird" or "totty." Apparently this called Bob's manhood into question, because he insisted I was wrong, calling me an idiot and a Limey. As he spoke he looked around to see if anyone else was hearing how clever he was. So I decided to be clever too. I announced I was going to the "loo" and I left the restaurant, leaving Bob to some other unfortunate Sheila, totty, or bird. ❤

Kristos, 21
Baker
MARRIED

This date was a real ego booster. His name betrayed Kristos's Greek heritage, although he had never been to Greece himself. He told me that his family liked to observe many Greek traditions, though he never told me what they were.

Why would a twenty-one-year-old answer my ad? For God's sake, he's only a baby. When I put the question to him, he told me he was lonely and he needed to get away from his bride of . . . eleven weeks! Is this one of the Greek traditions he mentioned?

We had to meet for lunch because he worked nights at a bakery. Kristos tried to come across all sophisticated, but it just wasn't working. He was a little boy in a big man's suit—literally. The suit he wore was borrowed from his father-in-law! He told me he loved older women; it always makes me feel ancient to hear that, but I'm sure he thought he was paying me a compliment. He said he and his wife were fighting constantly (God knows how they found the time, as he works nights and she works days). They also lived with her parents and her three siblings. Don't know how he could feel lonely with all that amount of company around, but apparently he did.

Let's review this date: Kristos is twenty-one, married, and living with the in-laws. Somehow he has had the nerve to borrow his father-in-law's suit to go on a blind date! So far, so good. But it gets better.

Kristos proposed that I take him out once a week for a meal—preferably Thursdays, as that was the day his wife went to nail technician classes. In return, he would have sex with me. I didn't bother to respond to this gracious offer. I just paid our bill, and when he asked me for five dollars to get home, I gave it to him.

Kristos thanked me profusely and offered to kiss me outside the restaurant, up against the wall! I told him that wouldn't be necessary. When he asked if I wanted to touch him "there," I promised I would call him at the bakery the next day, and fled. It hadn't entered Kristos's head that I didn't know the number or even the name of his place of work. ❤

Martin, 44
Federal Employee
MARRIED

Martin didn't mention he was married until we were having lunch, when he felt he "had" to tell me. He hoped I didn't mind and impressed upon me that he didn't want to speak badly of his wife, as if that made the fact that he was cheating a whole lot better! I asked why he had answered my ad in the first place, and his response (this ridiculous answer was used by quite a few of the men in this chapter) was that he heard my voice and just felt compelled to answer. This hardly explains why he was perusing the personal ads in the first place, and if my voice has such hypnotic powers, then some hotshot telemarketing firm should hire me and pay me a fortune.

Martin clearly felt a little ashamed; he hadn't met me to get reprimanded. He asked me if I was a decoy, and I answered truthfully that I was not. Then he asked if we could cut the date short, as he wasn't feeling well. Of course I had no problem with that, and we shook hands as he said, "Nothing happened, did it? We just had a drink, right?" I agreed that nothing had happened and left feeling quite certain that he wouldn't cheat again in a hurry. Bet he wished he hadn't given me his personal phone numbers, though! ❤

Paul, 38
Advertising Executive
MARRIED

Paul had flown to Miami earlier that day and had several meetings lined up, so he couldn't meet me until the evening. That was fine with me, as I was working on the suntan. He named a restaurant in a trendy part of town and was already there when I arrived. As he stood to greet me, I noticed how small he was—only about five feet two—but he was nice looking and appeared quite charming. (Don't worry; I have not forgotten that he is married.) He told me he had lived a lot of his life in Chicago and Dallas, but traveled extensively because of his job.

We had a delicious meal, and over dessert I asked why he'd answered my ad, since he was, after all, a married man. He took a gulp of his wine and told me he liked to wear women's underwear and his wife found it repulsive! He was desperate to find a woman who would empathize with him and perhaps even buy some for him (he'd pay). He didn't know why he did it; it just made him feel "real good." He leaned over to me and whispered that under his business suit he was wearing white panties and he really wished he could show me. I really wished he wouldn't! He asked if I was shocked and if it bothered me, to which I replied it wouldn't bother me as long as they weren't *my* white panties.

I thanked Paul for the date and decided to spend the rest of my evening shopping (not for panties, though), as that made *me* feel "real good." ❤

Gary, 39
Broker
MARRIED

This one mentioned that he was married on the phone, but he still wanted to meet me. Gary was a very attractive man—Italian-American, tall, dark, and then some! Over dinner he told me that he was on his second marriage, which was only six months young. What was wrong, I inquired. His wife was from the Middle East and very volatile; they fought all the time, he explained. She was now in another state, staying with some relatives, so he was here with me.

Gary was destined to be a cheater. He oozed charm and used it to the full effect. If he hadn't been a philanderer and I hadn't been writing this book, then I could definitely have got to grips with this man. He actually made my legs go weak at the knees. He spoiled it, though, by telling me he knew the effect he was having on me. I had to get away from him (I really did) and feigned a headache. He asked me not to send him away and said I would be sorry if I allowed him to leave. I secretly agreed, but nonetheless I chose to leave. Of all the men I had met, he was the only one to have that kind of effect on me, and I can see how easy it would have been to get involved with a man like him, only to have him break my heart. So ladies, to be safe, stay away from devastatingly good-looking men called Gary. ❤

Steven, 32
Corporate Wizard
MARRIED

I never did find out what a corporate wizard does, but I'd guess it's a profession that is much misunderstood, just like Steven.

Steven loved my accent (of course) and told me I sounded very sexy on the phone. Almost as soon as we met, he said he felt really comfortable with me and wrote down a series of telephone numbers, including his home number. (What a fool.)

While we sipped martinis at a very lovely bar, Steven told me he was "somewhat attached." What the heck does that mean, I asked. I helped him (and myself) out by saying, "So you're a married man, Steven?" To which he replied, "Yeah, kinda." He told me he was, of course, *unhappily* married, and I bet myself that he wouldn't last ten seconds before he started to trash his wife.

I had counted to nine when he said, "My wife is never home and she's always at her girlfriend's house and she never cooks or cleans the house." So why does he stay with her? Well he kinda loves her and they have a small child and on top of it all, he really cannot afford to leave. Big mortgage, car payments, all that good stuff. So he stays with her and cheats on her when he can. Lovely!

Apparently Steven felt he'd made his case, because he asked if I liked him. When I said, "No, I don't. You are nice to look at but your attitude towards your marriage stinks," he sat there with his mouth open and didn't even say anything as I got my coat and left. Reality soon sank in, though, because he came rushing after me and asked if he could please have the telephone numbers back.

No problem, Steven. ❤

Billy, 38
Teacher
MARRIED

Billy left a very funny message for me. He was very cheerful and sounded nice. But we all know how deceiving a nice voice can be, so I didn't have any expectations. I called him, and we arranged to meet the next day for dinner.

It took Billy right up until dessert to tell me he was married. He looked sheepish and said he was sorry. He didn't want to speak about his wife, neither in a good nor in a bad way, and he wouldn't explain why he'd answered my ad. (I think we can guess the answer to that one.) He shook my hand and said he was extremely sorry for deceiving me and for wasting my time. I acted suitably upset and our date was over. If only he knew. Maybe he will now. ❤

Mark, 32
Clothing Designer
MARRIED

"Have you heard the joke about the man who didn't wear underwear?" Mark asked when we spoke on the phone.

When I told him that I hadn't, he said, "It's not a joke, it's me!"

What was there to say but "Oh."

He went on to ask if we could meet for a drink so we could "talk about stuff." He liked the sound of me, apparently, and thought we might have something in common. God only knows what he could have had in mind. But I set off to find out.

Mark was a handsome man indeed, and full of compliments. He told me whom he worked for and whom his wife, whom he mentioned by name, designed for. Mark also showed me her photograph. She was a beautiful woman! All very nice so far.

As we sipped our drinks, I got around to asking him why he was dating in the personals when he was a married man with a lovely wife. His answer was, "I can't go out with anyone at work—they know my wife." But Mark didn't want to "get into all that stuff"; he just wanted to talk about his lack of underwear. Also he wanted to know if I liked to go out without panties.

Borrowing his reply, I told him that I didn't want to get into "all that stuff" either. He didn't like that and said, "Well, why are you here, then?" He had a point, so I decided to level with him. I told him that I was researching a book and he was going to be in it. How did he feel about that?

This man who wore no underwear told me that he was just acting the fool; he really did wear underwear, he said. (As if his lack of underwear was going to be his wife's premier concern, should she find out.) Mark informed me that he had to leave. He apologized to me and asked that I not contact him again. I promised him that he would never hear from me again. I didn't promise that I wouldn't write about him, though, so here he is.

Mark, the designer who likes to let it all hang free! ❤

Lance, 37
Marketing Executive
MARRIED

On the voicemail message Lance stated he was tall, athletic, handsome, had a good standard of living, and was married. He certainly looked the part when we met up in a South Beach restaurant for dinner. I got around to asking him why he was cheating on his wife, and he informed me that taking another woman to dinner was not cheating. I asked if his wife knew he was here with me. Of course she didn't. So in my book, that's cheating. Lance told me that if I played my cards right, he would show me what *real* cheating was all about. How could I resist such a charmer? I went to the ladies' room and didn't return, that's how. ❤

Mitchell, 46
Trucker
MARRIED

On the voicemail message that Mitchell left, he said he was a big guy and he used to be a "Green Bay Packer." As I'm from England, this meant nothing to me. I had visions of him boxing up some kind of green product.

We met up in a seafood restaurant in Fort Lauderdale. He was a big guy—not fat, just big—and he commented that he'd gained weight since he'd left the "Packers" some years back. I was still picturing a long line of guys packing, and like a fool I asked him what he'd packed. He looked at me in disbelief and explained that he didn't pack anything—he had played football! Oh well, that's sorted out, then. But I thought football players earned millions of dollars. Why was he working for the phone company? Apparently it's only the big stars that earn big bucks, as he explained it, and after you finish playing, you have to do something to pay the bills. And why was he meeting me when he was a married man? His wife was out of town visiting relatives and he got lonely. I suggested he "pack" his bags and go and join her. At that he laughed and said I was cute. Then he tried to feed me banana slices dipped in strawberry sauce.

End of date. ❤

Michael, 42
Construction Company CEO
MARRIED

"My wife's away and I'm ready to play." Those were the first words I heard from Michael. Now, if I had really been looking for a relationship, would I respond to such an obviously insensitive cheat? But he was number three, so off I went. He asked if I would meet him at his company apartment but accepted my refusal graciously, naming instead a restaurant that was well known for its seafood.

Michael was a very good-looking man, tall and smartly dressed. He acted pleased to see me and told me to order anything I wanted, as I was his guest. But when I asked why he had answered my ad, he refused to discuss it. He wasn't angry; he just didn't want to speak about it. Instead we spoke about our kids and our jobs. We acted as though we were old friends, and it was a very pleasant date. A bit bizarre, but nice.

Michael said he realized that his little quip about his wife being away had been flippant, and he apologized. He told me he was really looking for sex and he didn't want to lead me on in any way. (I must be a really good actress because I have all these married men apologizing to me for leading me on, when in fact it is the other way round!) He gave me a telephone number, a "very" private line that apparently only he answered, and asked me to call him the following day. He didn't make a fuss when I refused to give him my number. He came across as quite charming, and it's easy to see why women fall for guys like him. I know he was married, so for all his charm he's still a cheat. The only saving grace was he 'fessed up immediately. Not that that's any consolation, really—especially if you're his wife! ❤

Peter, 49
Lawyer
MARRIED

This man left a message on the voicemail saying he would be flying into the city on Wednesday and would love to meet up. He suggested a five-star restaurant and sang the praises of a particular dish it was supposedly famous for. When I arrived, Peter kissed my hand and ordered Champagne for us. He spoke of his delight at meeting me and told me how much he loved England and especially London. It would be very easy to mark Peter down as a real nice guy, and to me he was. But he was a married man, and no doubt his wife would not think so kindly of him. When he explained the reason for our meeting, it was plain and simple: He cheated because he could. I believed what he said, but it left a nasty taste. I decided to leave before the entrée. Why? Because I could! ♥

Marty, 53
Lawyer
MARRIED

Marty made a point of letting me know he was quite wealthy. He mentioned that he owned a home in the city and an estate in the suburbs and loved all the good things in life. (Apparently that doesn't include your wife, huh, Marty?) He didn't say too much about his looks, other than the fact that he had "a full head of silver hair." He asked if I liked Chinese food and suggested we meet for dinner the following evening at a Chinese restaurant he knew.

Marty was waiting for me in the lobby, and he greeted me by putting his hands on either side of my head and trying to kiss me on the mouth. In fact he only managed to kiss my left eyebrow, as I ducked away from his pursed lips. How extremely presumptuous of him! Now I was on my guard, so when we were shown to the table and he wanted to sit next to me and not opposite, I refused. This date was going downhill fast, and we hadn't even managed to sit down yet! But I decided he couldn't get up to much in a busy restaurant, so I tried to relax and enjoy the evening.

Wouldn't you know it, this man wanted to feed me. He picked up a sparerib and tried to put it in my mouth. Then he wanted me to eat from the same fork he was using. When I felt his sock-clad foot sliding up my leg and heading for my thigh, I knew I had to get out of there. I was out of the restaurant and in a cab in about twenty seconds, leaving Marty scrambling under the table for his shoe, which I had conveniently slid way across the restaurant. How was he going to explain that one, I wonder! ♥

Martin, 37
Florist
MARRIED

Martin didn't like to say he was married. He chose to say he had a "situation." Whatever! Doesn't matter how you twist it and turn it, married is married. Anyway, we decided to meet up for lunch in an Italian restaurant. When we sat down, Martin told me that he had never cheated before, but not because it was wrong or because he loved his wife. The reason he had remained faithful for six years was because of his ears! Apparently up until eight weeks ago Martin had had Prince Charles ears. Since he had undergone the operation to pin the flappers back, he told me he had gained confidence, had his hair cut short, and was scouring the personal ads. I was the first he had met. (Lucky old me.)

Martin asked if his "situation" bothered me, and I said yes. I thanked him for meeting me and at his insistence reassured him that it wasn't because of his ears that we wouldn't be seeing each other again. I watched him as he ambled down the street with a hand covering each ear, as if he were afraid they would fall off. What a "situation" *that* would be. ♥

Billy, 36
Internet Company CEO
MARRIED

Get a load of this guy! Billy was very professional on the phone. He told me he was "attached" but would really like to meet up. He described himself as very attractive and promised I "wouldn't be disappointed." (How many times had I heard that phrase!) Well, we did meet up in the bar of a well-known hotel, and I must be honest and tell you that he actually was a very good-looking man. He was tall, dark, and then some! But he had an ugly side to him.

Billy informed me, in a very businesslike way, that he and his "attachment" were trying to have a baby. It was very stressful because nothing had happened in three years and it was taking a toll on their relationship; she always seemed to be crying and it pissed him off! Sex with her had become so clinical that he felt an affair might help their relationship.

What was in it for me, I wondered aloud. Well, wouldn't you just know that this guy was going to please me for hours? Oh, was he going to take me clothes shopping? No, he was going to make love to me like I had never experienced before. When he asked me what I thought, I decided to take the easy way out. I simply said I didn't find him attractive. He finished his drink, told me I wasn't all that hot, and left.

I saw that Billy had left his credit card behind the bar to run a tab. I wished I had the guts to order some Champagne, but his poor wife had enough to contend with and I didn't want to cause her any more grief when she discovered a $150 bar bill. ❤

Paul, 40
Lawyer
MARRIED

Paul described himself as very tall and honest, a financially secure gentleman who was married and had no intention of leaving his wife. He wanted to meet up as he loved my accent (of course) and felt we might have something in common. He suggested a restaurant that I knew, and a date was set for lunch.

He *was* tall, that was true, but the rest I would find out later. He embraced me and said he liked my legs and my outfit. I said thank you, and thank you. When we sat down, he asked me how much I weighed and did I wear stockings or panty hose? I told him what he wanted to hear, and he ordered some wine without asking if I preferred red or white. He asked me to sit with my legs crossed and with the crossed leg wrapped around the uncrossed leg, which he thought was sexy. When I said it was uncomfortable, Paul laughed and said he could see I was going to be trouble. This man I've only known for five minutes wants me to be a contortionist and *I'm* trouble?

Paul's reasons for meeting me when he was a married man were typical: I need something more than I get from my marriage; I am searching for a woman who understands me to the fullest. . . . Then he pleaded with me to cross my legs the way he had asked me to earlier. I refused, and as I bid him adieu suggested he might get more joy from an out-of-work circus performer. Completely unfazed, he asked if he could have my tights to take home "for later." God only knows what *that* meant. ❤

Samuel, 48
Computer Consultant
MARRIED

The arrogance of this man was overwhelming. We had a brief telephone chat, during which he told me he had a wife and kids but it wasn't enough for him and he wanted more. He made excellent money, stayed in the finest hotels, and could afford the best, he said. We arranged to meet the following day. Initially he was angry that I wouldn't reveal my telephone number and became a little irate when I didn't allow him to send a car to pick me up. But he calmed down, and I told him I would be at the designated venue on time.

Samuel had chosen a very posh restaurant and was waiting for me in the foyer. He kissed me European-style and handed me his card. As soon as we were shown to our table, he kind of took over. "Okay," he demanded, "why are you here?" What? I asked if he had chosen to forget that he answered my ad. (Selective memory seems to affect lots of men these days.) He pooh-poohed my question and asked me again why I had met him, suggesting that my motive for having dinner with him was his affluence.

I decided he was going to get the full Monty, so I told Mr. Arrogance that I was researching a book. He just happened to be caller number three (they hate being described as "caller"), and there was no other reason I was there apart from the fact that I was about to embark on the Married section and he fitted right in. He went pale for a moment, then began to laugh, albeit nervously, and asked how the book was coming along. I told him it was getting there, and I asked if he would like to leave, as he didn't look very comfortable now that he was no longer in control. He declined my offer of a quick getaway, so as soon as I had finished my drink, I got up to leave. I handed him his business card, which he took like a shot, and suggested he be more careful next time he answers personal ads. After all, you never know whom you'll meet. ❤

Mike, 34
Engineer
MARRIED

This one used what he thought was a sexy voice to entice me to call him back. His message was full of *Mm-mmms* and the "Oh I'm hot just thinking about you, baby" type of crap. In between the *oohs* and *ahhs* he mentioned that he was married, but *so* unhappy and he really needed a "soft" woman.

I called him and we arranged to meet in a few days' time. Between that call and the appointed day, Mike called eleven more times, leaving supposedly sexy messages on my voicemail, blowing kisses into the phone, and working in a few more *oohs*.

When the day of the meeting arrived, I was pleasantly surprised to see that Mike was around five feet nine and quite handsome. But he insisted on acting like a fool. He continued to use this ridiculous voice every time he addressed me, although he spoke normally when he ordered the wine. But as soon as the waiter walked away, it was all "Mmmm baby, I'll bet you feel so soft and smooth mm mm mm." It was truly creepy.

As we drank our wine he asked me to kiss him, and he seemed quite offended when I refused. He and his wife had little in common, he said, and he felt very unloved. He had answered my ad looking for a little affection, and I was behaving extremely coldly towards him. He let me know that he wasn't happy. I let him know that I wasn't either, and I was ending the date. Mike then dropped the seductive tones and in his normal voice let me know that I was a bitch and thought I was better than he was because I was from England. I didn't bother to answer. I just mused at how quickly his demeanor changed when he didn't get his own way. ❤

Thomas, 40
Textile Company Owner
MARRIED

Thomas had had lots of affairs and wanted to make it clear to me that he was not going to leave his wife. In a very cute southern drawl, he explained to me that southern men don't leave their wives: They stray but they stay. It was just that he loved sex and he needed it more than his wife. She was a sweetheart but he needed something that he didn't get from her. Phew! What a confession before dinner!

Apart from his ugly attitude towards marriage, he was an attractive man. With his blue eyes, nice tan, and fit body, I could see that he would have no problem attracting the opposite sex—maybe even some of the same sex, who knows? But sex was the beginning and end of his conversation fodder.

He bored me to tears with accounts of all his affairs. I've never understood why men would think any woman would be thrilled to hear about a potential partner's sexual conquests. I was so bored that I started to count the seconds between the times he blinked. Eventually I realized that Thomas actually thought that we would sleep together after our date, and I was more than chuffed when I informed him that it wasn't going to happen, not that night or any other night!

Good ol' Thomas was very put out at my unwillingness to share in a night (minute?) of passion with him, and he told me that he would find someone else and then I would be sorry. Well, there's no answer to that, so I'll just bid y'all good-night! ❤

Terence, 40
Hotel Security Officer
MARRIED

I liked the message Terence left on my voicemail. He was polite and very informative listing his likes and dislikes. The fact that he was married didn't come up until later.

We met for dinner at a restaurant near the hotel where he worked. Terence was a very handsome man, tall, dark-skinned, with beautiful eyes. He obviously knew he was "all that" because he spent quite a lot of time dipping his head so as to catch a glimpse of his reflection in the mirror.

We ordered drinks, and Terence watched intently as I tried to sip mine through what I eventually realized was a swizzle stick. Then he spoke. He was married, he said. His wife was not his ideal choice of the perfect woman, but he wasn't about to leave her, as she was a good mother and a great cook. (Wow, wouldn't she be just thrilled by this description.) Sexually, however, she didn't do it for him. (Did he think I would?)

Apparently Terence's wife had had a very religious upbringing and considered sex a chore, not something to enjoy; consequently Terence didn't enjoy himself either—well, at least not with her. I wondered what else Terence was about to reveal to me, and I didn't have to wait long. Speaking very slowly, lingering on each syllable, he told me, "I . . . am . . . very . . . very . . . oral." I got the picture. Wife was a bit uptight and here was Terence wanting to go downtown and she wasn't having any of it, thank you very much. He went on to tell me that a lot of African-American men don't like to perform oral sex although they love to receive it. But he was different. He . . . loved . . . it. He asked what I thought. Truthfully, at that moment I was thinking of a good friend in London who would cheerfully have gone off into the sunset with Terence. Before I could answer, he told me how big his penis was (my friend would have paid for his flight to London) and how he could keep going for hours (better yet, he could fly first class).

Time out. I reminded myself that Terence was married, cheating on his wife, and talking about sex on the first date. Not good. He said he had to go back to his hotel for a few minutes and although I said I would wait, I didn't. I hailed a cab and spent the next ten minutes with *another* man who was extremely oral; that driver didn't shut up the whole way home. I heard all about Romania, his two daughters, and his wife who waited on him hand and foot. I was worn out when I got home. Two oral men in one night? I should be so lucky. ❤

Ted, 37
Furniture Upholsterer
MARRIED

I met Ted for lunch in a diner. He had wanted to get burgers and eat them in his van, but I insisted we eat at the restaurant. He told me he had to get back to work in forty-five minutes. He took care to tell me he didn't make much money and had three mouths to feed, so he couldn't pay for my lunch.

If I could compare Ted to someone famous, it would have to be Woody Allen, although Woody is better looking. Ted's wife was a horrible, terrible woman, he complained, but she was the mother of his kids. Besides, she was very homely and if he left her, she'd be alone forever. He wanted a better-looking woman to have sex with. Imagine my pride when he announced he thought I was okay! Who did this jerk think he was? He was as plain as can be, married, with the charisma of an insect and no prospects to match. Thank goodness his time was up and he had to go. You're *gone,* Ted! ❤

Dev, 42
Owner of Electrical Appliance Stores
MARRIED

Dev was dressed from head to toe in beige, just as he had said he would be, and as I arrived at the restaurant he had chosen for its proximity to his shops, I heard him talking very loudly on his cell phone. Dev had been in the States for twelve years, and lost no time in telling me about both of his shops. He sold televisions, cameras, VCRs and the all-important stun gun to tourists who shop on Orlando's International Drive. He told me his brother lived in London and had a little shop but he couldn't pay his bills, as everything in England was so expensive (I know). But Dev had no such worries. He said, "Look me, I got plenty, plenty money, big house I like it."

But Dev didn't like everything about his life; his wife had gone to visit her parents and hadn't returned for seven months. He then looked at my breasts and asked, "How much size titty? You got big ones, isn't it? I like it, and English women are easy, they like it, yes?"

He seemed surprised that I wanted to leave but handed me his card, and as we parted he called out, "Come into shop, I'll give you good price." I couldn't believe that he honestly thought I would discuss my breasts in return for a discount on a Walkman! ❤

Bruce, 51
Executive
MARRIED

On the phone Bruce let it be known that he was a wealthy man. He told me he stayed at the finest hotels, dined at the best restaurants, and traveled first class.

We met for dinner in a fine restaurant, and I couldn't help but note that Bruce wasn't at all the way he had described himself. He had lied about his height and his weight, and he may have had dark hair once but not now. He had none, dark or otherwise. He seemed very blasé about his lies, so I didn't say anything. I asked why he was answering my ad, and he shot back "Because I can."

Bruce was so rude to the waiter that I decided that I didn't want to stay for dinner, and I made my excuses. For some reason he seemed genuinely upset, although he hadn't been especially nice up to that point. I almost relented when he called the waiter a "faggot" for bringing him the wrong drink. I shook his hand and left. Shouldn't you be on your best behavior when you are out on a first date? Memo to Bruce's wife: You have my sympathy! ♥

Dave, 47
Teacher
MARRIED

The message on my voicemail was in the form of a rhyme.

Happiness and hugs are here for you,
Love and kisses for us two.
If these are some of the things you crave,
Then I suggest that you call Dave!

It was so corny that I almost violated my number-three rule, but I bit the bullet. Dave was so pleased I had called and asked if it was the rhyme that did it for me. I told him it was, and he asked if we could meet up for dinner. (I still wonder how all these married men can go gallivanting about in the evenings. I'd want to know where my husband was at nine or ten at night.)

He was a pleasant-looking man, around five feet eight, with glasses. Over drinks Dave poured out his heart to me. He had a sick wife, he said, and he couldn't have sex with her. She had been ill for many years and he had had several affairs. The last one had only recently ended as the woman had moved to another city. So he was looking for another lover. I told him I didn't fancy interviewing for the position of his "latest lover," which he deemed a shame, as he quite liked the look of me. Then he smiled and said, "Well, there's no point in having dinner together, is there? Good-bye." With that he was gone. No rhymes, no nothing. So Dave, here's one from me to you:

> Good-bye Dave, good riddance too,
> I had a horrid time.
> I pity your poor wife at home,
> I'm glad that you're not mine!

❤

Joe, 40
Musician
MARRIED

This man was very honest (and stupid) about his private life, sharing so many personal details that I found it quite strange. The number he had left for me to call him was the club where he worked. When I called, we chatted briefly and arranged a meeting for Monday afternoon, his day off.

I met Joe in a bar at one-thirty. By ten minutes to two

I knew his wife's name, her vital statistics, and where she and her sister worked. He also told me the size of his penis and the technique he utilized for keeping his erection! Then I was treated to delightful descriptions of all the women Joe had bedded throughout his twelve-year marriage. He had answered my ad because his last two conquests had been "fucking bitches" to get rid of. This time he wanted to find someone who wasn't from his neighborhood— someone, he said, who didn't know "a whole lot" about him. Had he forgotten the complete rundown I had just been treated to?

I finished my drink and told him I didn't think we were suited to one another, to which this prize of a man replied that if I had ten minutes with him, I would be "singing a different song." By then I knew everything I needed to know about Joe . . . and then some. ❤

Carl, 37
Salesman
MARRIED

All Carl wanted, he claimed, was a woman he could have oral sex with. How about that woman you walked down the aisle with, that one who wore the white dress, I wondered. At our meeting in a Mexican restaurant, he told me his wife didn't like oral sex and he loved to "orally please." Was he really just looking for a woman he could perform oral sex on? Yes, he assured me he was. Selfless as his offer was, I told him I must decline.

His urge to do this was so strong, Carl explained, that he had begun to visit prostitutes. But he was curious as to why I wasn't interested. After all, he was an attractive man, wasn't he? He didn't want intercourse, just to please me. I thanked him but again declined the offer. Carl shook my hand and walked out of the restaurant, looking very dejected.

It was all so businesslike, so clinical. I guess he felt that if it was just his tongue that was involved, and not his emotions, then it was okay. What do you bet his wife would have another take on it? ❤

cops and robbers

I didn't get a lot of calls in this category, but the messages I received from prison inmates certainly made a big impression. One incarcerated soul called eleven times to ask if I'd visit him. His offense was nonviolent in nature, he explained, but I needed to call his mother's house so she could get the paperwork sorted out. Another wanted me to send him sexy letters for him to fantasize to. This is the only time I went against my "delete, delete, meet" rule, figuring that the prison gates were the right place to draw the line.

I did meet some men who were familiar with the "big house," though. A couple were correction officers, three were recent parolees, and one was out on bail awaiting trial—and fully expecting to be convicted. Except for one who was accused of double murder, all of them were at pains to tell me that any crimes they had been accused of were nonviolent, and almost all of them claimed to be innocent. Needless to say, I approached these dates with even more than the usual caution.

That said, these were far from the worst of the lot. What girl doesn't feel safe when her date is packing a sidearm (or wearing an electronic monitoring bracelet)? And at least you'll always know where your man is at night if he's serving ten to twelve.

Spencer, 33
Salesman
SINGLE

Spencer kept his past a secret until we met, but after a few glasses of wine he told me that he'd answered my ad because he'd only just been released from prison. He wanted me to know that he'd been incarcerated for three years due to Mayor Koch and a gun! He was anxious to go into the details: Several years previously, someone had stolen a gun and hidden it in the car Spencer owned. The police found the gun when they pulled him over for a routine speeding ticket. As he was the owner of the car, Spencer went to jail.

He didn't seem unhappy or bitter, and after sharing that initial bit of personal information he went on to speak about other things. Spencer told me he'd had a girlfriend when he was sent to jail, but she had become tired of waiting for him and they had split up. He had a job selling shoes now, and he had kept the apartment he'd rented before the jail term (a friend had paid the rent for him).

I asked Spencer why he'd told me about his prison term, to which he replied that he'd wanted to be honest with me from the start. That could have been my cue to come clean with him and tell him that I was just doing research for my book, that I didn't really want to meet anyone for a long-term relationship. But I was too nervous, so I kept quiet and decided not to share in this honesty moment we were having. Spencer was happy to do all the talking, anyway, and I nodded in all the right places and laughed at his jokes, which were indeed very funny. At the end of our date he gave me a kiss on the cheek and said he'd leave it up to me to be in touch with him.

Two weeks later, Spencer called the voicemail and left a message asking if I would give him a call as he wanted to invite me to a fancy ball for which he had tickets. I called him back and when his machine came on, I came clean and told him about my book. I said it was very nice of him to invite me but I wasn't interested.

Several days later Spencer left another message on my voicemail. He said he never wanted to see me again, and the only reason he'd invited me to the ball was because his first choice had been unavailable. I was very pleased that I was in a different state when I heard his message—and also glad that I hadn't been brave or silly enough to tell him about my book on our date. Lesson learned. ❤

Arthur, 34
Parolee
SINGLE

Arthur was the first man I'd met who wore a tag. No, not one of those expensive watches, but a tag on his ankle! He explained that he'd just been released from jail and the tag wearing was part of his parole. He hadn't mentioned anything about his anklet on the phone, but I suppose it's not the sort of thing you would brag about.

Arthur had owned a computer company before going to jail and he still had it, so he wasn't down on his luck at all. He assured me that he wasn't a violent man and explained that he had been incarcerated for fraud. Arthur admitted his guilt and said that he was now paying the price for his wrongdoing.

Arthur was a natty dresser and the tag was quite well hidden under his Versace pants and socks. He was also extremely good looking, and charming too.

We ordered a drink. (He couldn't drink alcohol, so we had soda.) Arthur said that he had only mentioned his tag in case I had wanted to go somewhere else after our dinner. He could only travel a certain distance from his house before the tag would start to beep!

We had a very nice dinner. I felt perfectly comfortable with Arthur, and he was a superb conversationalist. As the evening drew to a close, Arthur asked if I would like to see him again, but before I could answer, he said he didn't want to embarrass me and handed me a card with all of his numbers on it. Then he called a taxi for me and said he would wait inside the restaurant so I would feel safe and could see that he wasn't trying to follow me.

I don't suppose it took him long to get home; he could only travel a few hundred yards before he would begin to beep.

Arthur was one of my most eloquent dates and I almost feel bad putting him in this section, because in all ways but one he was a 10/10 date. In different circumstances, I would probably have called him again. But I had a job to do, and a man with a tag was not on the agenda! No offense, though, Arthur. Well, only the fraud! ❤

Edward, 37
Car Salesman
SINGLE

When Edward and I met, he told me that he had answered quite a few personal ads in his time and he had even placed his own a couple of years ago. Things hadn't worked out as he'd hoped (the only replies he'd received were from prostitutes), so when he'd seen my ad he decided to take a chance and call.

Edward was a nice-looking man. He was very tall and quite a head-turner with his dark, wavy hair. The only turn-off note was a strong smell of mothballs.

We chatted for a while, and Edward offered an assurance that he liked me. Then he said that he wanted to tell me something. I mentally gave Edward ten out of ten for his staying power; it had been almost an hour before he had felt the urge to confess what I expected to be a sexual fantasy, probably involving the aforementioned mothballs. I braced myself for what I was about to receive, and Edward announced that he was awaiting sentencing on drug charges.

It wasn't a big deal, apparently; he was only expecting a short incarceration period. He then winked at me and said, "Do you want a line? I have got the best shit, I'm telling you. This will blow your head off."

I didn't want anything that would blow my head off, thank you very much, and told him so. He appeared surprised and said, "You were sniffing a lot. I thought you were suffering from Colombian flu, if you know what I mean."

I toyed with the idea of telling him that my sniffing was due to his musty mothball stench, but decided against it. After all, he was a drug dealer and didn't they carry weapons in their socks? I've seen *Cops*, I know what goes on!

Edward encouraged me to have a little coke and loosen up, and then he let it go, saying, "I'm going to have some and then we'll be on different levels."

Obviously he didn't realize that we already were. When he went to the bathroom to do his snorting, I went to the door to do my leaving! 💙

Larry, 33
Law Enforcement Officer
SINGLE

I liked Larry. He'd laughed when I said that I'd expected him to take me to Dunkin Donuts for our date as if he hadn't heard it a thousand times before. We actually met up in a Red Lobster. While we ate, Larry told me that he'd lived in Miami all his life and he loved it; he'd never live anywhere else. He asked a lot of questions about me, and we had a pleasant date. He said he'd answered my ad because he found it difficult to meet women outside the police force.

It was a first for me to have a date with a man packing a pistol. As I looked around the restaurant, in fact, I noticed quite a few of Miami's finest dining there. Well, at least you felt safe; it was hardly likely to be robbed while half the police force was having fish and chips. Larry was the only date I allowed to walk me to my car. If you can't trust a policeman . . . ❤

Stan, 33
Law Enforcement Officer
MARRIED

Stan didn't mention in his message that all he wanted to do was a little bit of role-playing. He was a medium-size man, with fair hair and red cheeks. Over dinner in a Chinese restaurant, he asked what kind of things I liked to do for fun. I answered ice skating, traveling, and reading. When I asked him the same question, Stan told me that he liked to make believe that he was a "sales clerk in a convenience store"! I wondered why he found that quite so appealing, and he replied that it made him feel "superior" knowing that he had items that others wanted.

It's strange for a policeman to want to play-act at being a sales assistant. Obviously there had to be a sexual motive. Stan admitted to me that the thought of standing behind the cash register, especially if it was on a higher level than the customer, was a major turn-on for him. He asked if I thought we could get this little scenario going. I had to say no. I found the whole idea hysterical. If I did want to play his game, I would have to pretend to be the customer and buy stuff. How is that exciting? It's what I do every day! I suggested that he get a part-time job in a store as a way of making this fantasy real for him. Stan explained that he wasn't allowed to moonlight, and anyway, he'd be so turned on, he wouldn't get any work done.

As I walked away from the restaurant after our meal, I noticed the sign on a police car that said, "TO SERVE AND PROTECT." Well, at least Stan was halfway there. ❤

George, 55
Transport Company Owner
SINGLE

George had committed fraud on rather a large scale. His crime had to do with the IRS, and his explanation was quite intricate. I don't know why he chose to tell me about it, as I otherwise would never have known. George had spent "too much time in jail, baby" and he wasn't going back. I was glad to hear it. He wore a smart business suit and took several calls on his cell phone before turning it off so we could get to know each other without interruptions.

Apparently George didn't have a lot of luck with the ladies. He told me that two of his wives had cleaned him out and the other two had left him. That's why he had started looking through the personal ads. He didn't want a relationship. Women were trouble. He must have seen the worried look on my face because he reached for my hand and told me he was only joking. (If only he'd known how mutual the feeling was.) Then the conversation shifted to his children. He had eight, and they were costing him a fortune in school fees.

When we left, I thanked him for meeting me and he asked if perhaps we could get together another time. I said "Mmm," as I didn't want to say yes or no. He seemed happy with "Mmm," so all was well. He said he'd had a good time and had enjoyed meeting me. I had to agree that I had had a good time too, and it was a pleasure to meet him. I doubt that the IRS thought so highly of him, though! ❤

Freddie, 46
Just Rich
SINGLE

This is a terrible tale, and one that really shook me up. Freddie and I met up in a wonderful Southern restaurant for lunch. He hadn't told me too much about himself on the phone, but he was very polite and he did mention that he was lonely. To cut a long date a little shorter, Freddie said that he had been on death row, falsely accused of double homicide. He had recently been released and had won financial compensation for his wrongful imprisonment. He said his family had deserted him during his incarceration, but now that he had money they were calling again and he didn't want anything to do with them.

When I asked him if he'd tell me how he came to be charged with a crime of such magnitude, he obliged and gave me the full details. He also apologized for his lack of manners, saying he'd been out of circulation a long time, but he needn't have—his manners were fine. (In fact, they were a lot better than some of the dates that had never been to jail.)

I really felt for Freddie, and I knew that I had to tell him the truth about my own motives for being there. Fortunately he took it very well, and we spent at least an hour talking about some of the quirkier men I had met. When our date came to an end, I didn't know what to say to him, so I wished him well and I promised I would send him a copy of my book when it came out. As I watched him drive off in a Mercedes Benz, I chatted with the waitress, who was amazed at the generous tip he had left.

When I told a friend about this date, she was skeptical about his story and thought it may well have been just that—fiction. She felt sure there would have been some press coverage about Freddie being released and thought that I should check him out. I haven't and I won't. If he was lying, then he really took me. If he was telling the truth, then I do wish him well. I still think about him today and wish him only the best. ❤

Kenny, 40
Graphic Artist
SINGLE

When Kenny and I met up, he told me that he had just been released from prison. Had I known that before-hand, I doubt we would have gotten together. Kenny had spent five and a half years in prison for illegal possession of a gun. Now I, being English, thought everyone in America had a gun (didn't you go to jail here for *not* possessing a weapon?).

Kenny was soft spoken and nice looking and wanted to know all about me, but something about him made me uneasy, so I made up a lot of nonsense, including the fact that I would probably be going back to London very soon. He told me that he loved my accent, and for once I didn't get smart like I usually do. I like to tell people that they are the ones with the accent, not me, but on this occasion I decided to be gracious, or perhaps cautious, and accept his comments with a smile. He showed me some of his artwork, and it was really quite spectacular. After we'd had a couple of drinks, Kenny suggested that we call it a night. Was an ex-con dumping me? Apparently Kenny was concerned that I was feeling uncomfortable with him. Polite *and* astute! ❤

Chris, 33
Prison Guard
SINGLE

Chris was the most racist person I have ever met in my life. I don't know why it is that some people feel it's perfectly okay to inflict their poisonous views on listeners simply because we have the same skin color. I listened as this crew-cut neo-Nazi made vulgar comments about everyone who passed by. While I agree that the inmates in the jail where he worked may not have been role models, they *were* human.

I'm not going to devote too much space to this monster. It's enough to say that he is the exact stereotype of a racist Southern prison guard. After forty minutes I told him that I really didn't agree with his views and I preferred not to hear them. He asked if I was a "n***** lover," and said that if I was, then he didn't want to see me again. He continued that he'd had bad vibes about me from the beginning and I'd most likely be all over him if his name was Leroy and he played basketball. I looked at him for just a second, then said, "Yeah, most likely," and left. ❤

Tony, 45
Furniture Mover
SINGLE

When I listened to the message Tony left for me, I could hardly understand him. I later discovered that he was a native New Yorker who spoke extremely fast and didn't finish off all of his words. He commented that the way I spoke was fine for me, but when Englishmen spoke they sounded gay. Such criticism from a man whose very favorite expression was "A yoo kiddin' me swee-har"? Everything I said seemed amazing to him, and he often repeated this favorite phrase.

Tony wasn't a bad-looking guy. He wasn't a very good citizen, though. I have him in this section because he was out on bond and fully expecting to go to jail when he went back to court. I have listed Tony's occupation as "furniture mover," but in fact he moved the furniture out of people's houses when they weren't home. Only rich people, mind you, and he had been pretty good at his job until he got caught.

We were having dinner in a restaurant that Tony had chosen, and I noticed that he was extremely well known there and the food was excellent. It seemed that every ten minutes somebody came by the table to say "How you do-in?" He was happy to tell me that the reason he answered my ad was because he was looking for "a little somtn noo." (That's "something new" for those uninitiated to New York–speak.)

Tony figured that if he were to be jailed, he'd be sent to a place in New Jersey called Rahway. He took great pains to tell me where it was and that Sylvester Stallone had filmed a movie there called *Lockdown*. He had a friend who was doing time there when the movie was being made, and they used some of the inmates as extras. He asked if we could keep in touch when he was incarcerated, and if I could spare the time would I visit sometimes? What he actually said was "I could tell the guys a British piece a ass was coming." Ah, such a way with words.

As our date came to an end, Tony kissed my hand and thanked me for meeting him. I offered to pay half, and of course "Yoo kiddin' me swee-har" was uttered. He gave me a business card (a thief with his own business card) and asked for my address so he could write to me, but he understood when I was reluctant to give out that information. I left the restaurant with a very full tummy.

I really would like to go back to that restaurant, but I don't want to bump into Tony. Well, at least not with another date, anyway. Can you imagine it: "Yoo writin' a book, yoo kiddin' me swee-har." I guess I'll have to delay returning there until he's gone to jail. By the way, does anyone know how much time you get for stealing rich people's furniture? ❤

Martin, 33
Corrections Officer
MARRIED

The restaurant where Martin and I met was one I'd been to the previous day with another date, and the hostess recognized me and greeted me like a long-lost friend. Martin was already there and stood to greet me and shook my hand. He had mentioned on the phone that he was tall, but not that he was basketball-player Shaq-type tall—he must have been seven feet.

After we ordered drinks, Martin told me how unhappy he was at home. (Because he couldn't fit into it?) He told me his wife was the problem! Surprise, surprise—she was a bitch and all she did was bitch at him. (She'd bitch a lot more if she knew he was out answering ads.) But he did love his kids and he couldn't afford a divorce. He put in for as much overtime as he could get so he didn't have to spend too much time at home. He spoke a lot about his job, and that's the only time during our meeting that he smiled or livened up at all.

On my way home I got to thinking that Martin's marriage really must be over if he preferred the company of convicted felons to that of his wife, and male felons at that. If his wife ever wanted a divorce, she could cite cellblock C as co-respondent! ❤

Bill, 33
Corrections Officer
SINGLE

Bill looked exactly like a wrestler from the World Wrestling Federation. He was big—very big. He had a crew cut and turned up to meet me in his uniform, saying, "Women love my tight pants. Don't you?" He was too big to disagree with, so of course I told him that I did. As he was off "dooty" he could have a drink, and drink he did! The waiter was on permanent call to our table. Never mind that it was "happy hour"; for Bill it was ecstatic hour. It seemed that every minute he was yelling "Scotch rocks" and yet another drink would appear. I, on the other hand, intended to stay very sober around this guy.

Bill insisted upon telling the two guys at the next table that I was from London, and when he pronounced the word "London," he would tilt his head back and raise his chin and glass in what could only be a misguided attempt at being funny. After a few more drinks, he told the new people next to us (the others had moved) that he had "found me in a personal column and that I was begging for it." Immediately I picked up my bag and made for the door. He was so inebriated that he assumed I was going to the ladies' room. "Do one for me, baby," he called. I did one for him, all right. I did one more step that took me right out the door. ❤

___

Melvin, 37
Law Enforcement Officer
SINGLE

From the moment we met, Melvin was at great pains to convince me that he was a legitimate law enforcement officer. He wasn't like a security guard, he was a *real* policeman, with a *gun*. Then this "policeman" proceeded to tell me that he could get any drug I wanted. I told him thanks, but no thanks.

He wasn't in uniform, when we met, but he did show me some kind of ID that looked official. When I showed disdain for his talk of narcotics he switched his demeanor, claiming he'd mentioned drugs just to see if I was "into the drug thing," and if I had been then he would have left and our date would have ended. See, it was a trick! Ooh, how clever he was. I considered changing my mind now and asking if he could "score a gram of coke" as he attempted to impress me with tales of his escapades on the police force. He seemed especially eager to show me his gun, as he knew that policemen in England don't carry weapons. The gun was in his jacket but he didn't want to get it out in the restaurant; he said he would show it to me later at his apartment.

Let me get this straight. This complete stranger expects me to accompany him to his apartment, where he will show me his gun. Is that one hell of an offer or what? He then told me he had three other weapons at his home, at least one of which was deadly. I had no qualms whatsoever about going to the ladies' room and skipping out on this one. I jumped into a cab and counted myself lucky to have escaped, though I didn't think he would actually do anything worse to me than bore me to death.

Melvin was no more a police officer than I was. ❤

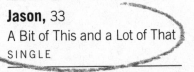

Jason, 33
A Bit of This and a Lot of That
SINGLE

Jason wanted to meet in the restaurant of a certain top-notch hotel, as that's where he was staying for a couple of days. When I arrived, he ran over and swung me around, to the bemused looks of the other guests. "I like it, I like it," he said as he looked me over. "Come on, let's go to the bar!" With that, he took my hand and whisked me off to the bar area, ordering a glass of wine for me, as he had a drink already.

I asked what he meant when he said his job was "a little bit of this and a lot of that." Jason wouldn't tell me. He put his finger to his nose and then said, "If I tell ya, I'll have to kill ya." Then he laughed and put his arm around me, as if to let me know he was joking, adding, "I just got out of jail. Don't fret, it wasn't a violent offense and I've made a lot of money."

Jason had a briefcase with him, and inside he had a bottle of liquor. With the exception of our table the bar was almost empty, so Jason had no problem taking the bottle out and showing it to me. He poured a little into each of our glasses.

This drink was called absinthe and apparently it was illegal in America. He had managed to get ahold of it, and he wanted me to try some. Jason said, "It will blow your head off. Sip a little and then we'll go dancing." Was this guy crazy? He wants me to try a drink that's banned in the U.S. and then, while I am "out of my head," to trust my life to a complete stranger? I don't think so, Jason! He was getting very drunk now, continuing to sip the absinthe while telling me how wonderful it was. I could see that it was very powerful liquor, as Jason was giggling about like a fool.

That was my cue to go to the ladies' room and do a detour to the exit. Within two minutes, I was in a cab and on my way home. Sorry, Jason, but I'm not convinced that absinthe makes the heart grow fonder. ❤

sad sacks and losers

There are as many legitimate reasons for smart, funny, attractive men to place personal ads as there are for smart, funny, attractive women to answer them, and we all know someone who met his or her soulmate through some anonymous forum.

And then there are the guys who stand the best chance of getting a date with someone who knows little or nothing about them. These guys are chronically depressed, habitually in disarray, or totally deluded about their appeal to the opposite sex. Some seem unaware of just how sad they seem; others seemed to wallow, nay revel in their misery. Dating these men can be summed up in one word: downer.

The guys in this chapter went for the sympathy vote with me. Or they found the need to tell me very personal details about their very private parts. Still, all in the name of research, I met them and here they are. Losers? I'll let you judge for yourself.

Ray, 40
Bank Teller
MARRIED

We are allowed to forgive Ray for meeting me because although technically married, his wife had run away with a neighbor three weeks earlier. She told him she was going to the store to buy diapers and called him two days after the shopping trip to say she wasn't coming home, so he knew there was no foul play involved. But what was involved was another man, as if we didn't know!

I felt a bit sorry for Ray. He wasn't the best-looking man in the world and he had extremely yellow teeth. He was in complete denial about his wife having run away; he was under the impression that this neighbor had *stolen* his wife from him. Theft of a wife? Now you can steal a man's car, or his money maybe, but you can't steal a wife. They have to want to go.

But Ray was adamant that his wife had been stolen, bless him. He showed me her photograph, and to be honest, she didn't look like the kind of woman men would fight over. But who knows? Maybe she had hidden talents!

I asked if she had taken the baby with her. Ray told me that they didn't have any children. So who was she buying diapers for on that fateful night? He didn't know! Ray was seriously in denial here.

We had been on our date for over two hours when Ray told me that he was having a great time. He liked the fact that he could talk to me, he said.

Just as I was pondering how to end the date, Ray stood up and said, "I have to go now. Thanks for coming, but I have another date. Sorry I can't stay longer. I'll call you, though."

With that, he was gone.

Thank goodness. But I got to thinking that if Ray had spent half the time with a therapist that he had with me, it would have cost him a hundred bucks or more. As it turned out, it didn't cost him a penny, as he took off without paying the check or even offering to go dutch!

Ah well, Ray played me for a fool—or for a shrink! ❤

Casey, 36
Entrepreneur
MARRIED

Casey and I had a quick chat on the phone, during which he asked if we could meet that very evening, as he was leaving town early the next day. I agreed. Having declined his offer to send his driver to pick me up, I caught a cab to the designated spot. During the ride, my driver felt the need to share with me the fact that he hadn't been to the bathroom in seventeen hours. Not surprisingly, I didn't ask why. I certainly didn't want to hear the details.

When I reached the restaurant Casey was there, waiting for me. He kissed my hand, told me that I was lovely, and added that his penis was getting hard already, just at the sight of me. I turned right around and hailed a cab. What do you know? It was my haven't-been-to-the-toilet-in-seventeen-hours friend. After a quick deliberation, I decided that risking hearing why he hadn't pooped for so long would be more interesting than hearing the crap that Casey was doling out, so into the cab I went. At least I only had to suffer him for five minutes.

Casey called the voicemail and apologized for being obnoxious but said I should be flattered that I had made him horny. In fact he was feeling horny again. That was some apology . . . *not*! ❤

Kevin, 39
Realtor
MARRIED

When we spoke on the phone, Kevin told me he was married but he "wanted a little something more." Although I didn't know it at the time, he had already had that. Kevin and I met up the next day in a tapas bar, where they sell "little" dishes of food. (You'll get it in a moment, I promise.) He was a tall man, balding, with a serious face. He shook my hand and led me to a table, where he ordered a bottle of Zinfandel and then just looked at me. I asked if he was okay, to which he nodded but didn't say anything. When the wine arrived, he took a couple of sips and then promptly leaned forward and told me about his "little" problem, which he said was quite "embarrassing" and he didn't want anyone else to hear. Yeah, right. In a low voice Kevin confided that he had had a penile implant, but that the extra two inches were noticeable only when his penis was flaccid. It looked the same when it was erect. No one got to see how Dicky-doo had grown—no one except his wife, that is (surely she is the one who matters, Kevin).

Kevin asked if I would look at his penis while it was "soft" and tell him what I thought of it. What, here? Now? His serious face was even more serious now, and I could tell he wasn't joking. I gently offered that perhaps that was more appropriately a second-date activity. But he insisted that he wanted my opinion that very night. He suggested we go sit in his car and do it, and had the audacity to become angry when I refused. Call me old-fashioned, but *no*. I wanted to leave, so I asked for the check. Promptly Kevin told me off for belittling him. I laughed at his unfortunate choice of words—I couldn't help myself.

As we walked out of the restaurant I saw a gentleman I knew from my hotel and stopped to make small (sorry, Kevin) talk. Kevin pushed past me, calling me a "little bitch." Not just a bitch, but a *little* bitch. My friend asked what that was all about and I was going to tell all, but I changed my mind and decided to head home. The stress of that date had made me hungry. I stopped on the way home for a hot dog—a foot-long, of course. ❤

Derek, 38
Told Me He Was Disabled
MARRIED

Get your handkerchiefs out for this guy; he was full of tragedy and woe. Within minutes of meeting Derek I heard that:

1. He had walked through a glass door and almost bled to death.
2. A year later he had a serious car accident, and he was now in the process of getting a big settlement.
3. His toenails fell off and wouldn't grow back.
4. He slept with a gun for fear of intruders.

After hearing his sad story, I wondered why he was here with me; didn't he have enough on his plate without cheating on his wife? Well, yes, it would seem that way. But Derek had a further cross to bear. It seems he and his wife didn't have sex anymore because:

1. She had a demanding job and had women's problems.
2. Her father was living with them and it made things difficult.

How much more tragedy was this man about to unload on me? More, much more. But I won't depress you as he did me. Let's cut to the chase: Derek wanted extramarital sex, and he wanted it with me. Well, maybe I wasn't his first choice, but I was the only one there. He looked beseechingly at me and asked if I felt sorry for him. I told him that if all he'd told me was true (it wasn't), then it was indeed very unfortunate. But I wasn't in the habit of getting naked with everyone who fed me a sob story. He asked if I had a friend he could meet, if I wasn't interested. I couldn't think of anyone that I disliked enough to unloose on Derek. So we parted amicably. ♥

Phil, 50
Manufacturer
MARRIED

I met Phil at a very expensive restaurant in the city. He had wanted to meet up at 4:00 P.M. but I couldn't make it until 6:30. When I arrived he was intoxicated, and he stumbled as he stood to greet me. I decided one of us needed to keep a clear head and ordered orange juice, to which he said, "I'm not buying orange juice. Get a shot of vodka in it." Without Phil noticing, I signaled the waiter to skip the shot, so all was well for a while.

Soon Phil began to trash his wife because of her weight, and when I told him I wasn't interested, he put his chin down onto his chest and pouted. Using what I'm sure he thought was a cute voice, he looked up at me and said, "Don't scold me. I've had a hard life." Then my drunken date proceeded to tell me in precise detail how he'd got where he was today. He was getting all teary-eyed. I, on the other hand, was getting ready to leave. When I told Phil I was going, he stood up, closed his eyes, and leaned over to me for a kiss. Goodness knows how long he stood there before he fell over! ♥

Kirk told me that he was married, and he also told me that he was very "big down there" and he wasn't referring to Australia!

What he failed to inform me of was his foul-smelling breath. The evil odor hit me the moment we met. As he said "Hello," I was knocked for six by the smell of three-day-old cabbage and bad eggs left in the pan too long. When he stepped closer, as if to kiss me, I involuntarily stepped back, right onto a female diner's foot!

We were shown to the table almost immediately, and I felt a little safer as I was opposite him and could keep my distance. But his breath wafted across the table to my poor nose whenever he spoke.

I decided that I should do a lot of the talking and steer Kirk away from using words that began with the letter "H," which propelled the stench towards me that much quicker. Alas, Kirk wanted to know all about me. "*How* long have you been in the United States?" "*How* do you like it here?" "*Who* else have you met?"

I was finding it difficult to disguise the fact that his bad breath was making me feel sick, but I didn't have the heart to tell him how I was actually feeling. So this ended up being one married man I never bothered to ask my standard question: Why was he cheating? In fact his breath saved him from having to answer *any* questions I may have wanted to ask. I also never told him that I was researching a book.

I couldn't bear the thought that he might be angry and say things like "*How* could you?" or "*Who* are you?"

So I just shook his hand and said good-bye, making it very clear that I would get the check and that he would be getting absolutely nothing. ♥

Raymond, 68
Furniture Company Owner
MARRIED

Raymond and I met for lunch in a hotel on the beach. He wore a suit, but the pants were shorts and he sported a pair of yellow socks that matched his toupee. He told me he'd answered my ad because his wife had gone up north to visit family and he wanted some company. I thought that a man of sixty-eight would have been happy with TV for company, but who knows what the Miami sunshine does to a man, or maybe he'd been at the Viagra.

Anyway, Raymond said he was from New York and had lived in Miami for twelve years, and he loved it. He liked to walk on the beach and watch the women in their bathing suits. He especially liked European women, as some of them took their tops off and he could see their breasts. I knew the next question would be "Do you go topless on the beach?" so I beat him to it and told him I didn't. Then I steered the conversation back to him and why, at his age, he wanted to cheat on his wife. There were little drops of spit on either side of his mouth as he told me he had cheated on his wife throughout their marriage but it didn't mean he didn't love her. And he wasn't about to stop until the great man upstairs decided to take him. Funny he would mention God and having an affair all in the same sentence. I looked at the globs of spit and decided I'd had enough. Fortunately Raymond wasn't eager to prolong our meeting. He winked at me and said he liked me, but he was hoping to meet someone a little younger! ❤

William, 36
Broker
MARRIED

William greeted me warmly, in fact much too warmly. He hugged me as though we were long-lost lovers. He pushed his whole body towards me and I backed away as much as I could. When we sat down, he wanted to hold my hand. With his free hand he tried to stroke my hair and my face! Yuck!

Fortunately he sensed my dislike of this over-the-top display of affection and asked if he should stop. When I told him yes, he asked why I was acting so cold towards him. After all, didn't women complain all the time that men weren't loving and affectionate enough? I agreed, thinking that might well be the case from his wife's point of view anyway. It seems that William's wife had found out that William had been a bit too friendly with a coworker. Since that discovery, she had banished William to the spare room and only allowed him in the master bedroom when *she* desired sex!

The strange—or should I say stranger—part of this story is this: William said he didn't particularly enjoy intercourse; he liked to kiss and cuddle. That's all he had been participating in with the coworker, nothing more than that! I looked at him as he was telling me this, and I really couldn't make him out. He was quite nice looking, but he had a pathetic air about him. He was all doe-eyed and "silly boy lemon."

He cocked his head to one side and asked, "Why can't I find the woman who will love me for my gentleness? I only want intimacy from hugs, not full sex." He was looking at me now with "Lamb Chop" eyes, and his mouth turned down at the corners as if he was willing himself not to cry. "Love me for me," he whimpered. "I need you." What he needed was a kick up the backside, but I didn't tell him that for fear he would break down in tears.

I told William that I had to leave and that he should go home to his wife. At that he became angry. "You don't know what she's like. She lashes out at me. I've had bruises and bites from her." Then, almost as if a light bulb had switched on inside his head, he had what he decided was a "great idea."

That idea involved little old me paying a visit to his wife

and explaining that William needed more cuddles, which was why he had "contact" with other women!

I stood up and put on my coat. William stood too and engulfed me in a hug, rubbing his hands up and down my arms and shaking his head, muttering, "Don't leave me. Don't go." I was eventually able to peel him off.

Two days later, William left a message on the voicemail saying how much he missed me and could we please meet up again for some "intimacy." Intimacy? More than anything, he needed therapy. ❤

Carl, 45
Stockbroker
MARRIED

Carl's message gave me the distinct impression that he was feeling very sorry for himself, and trying to get me to feel sorry for him too. He said he was unhappily attached (there's that word again), and although he earned good money, his wife took it all. Wow, what a great catch: Not only is he married, he's poor too. How could he afford to have an affair, I wondered. We had a brief chat on the phone and arranged to meet for lunch that afternoon. He chose a very nice restaurant, so I guessed I was "expenses."

Sorry to say, but Carl was not a very nice-looking man. He wore the biggest glasses in the world and a continual frown. He shook my hand and began to tell me his woes, and believe me, this guy had woes with a capital W. Financially he was a disaster; he lived way beyond his means and his mother-in-law was about to move in with them. I tutted and uh-huhed in what I hoped were all the right places as he ran his fingers through the three or four hairs still left on his head. He didn't know how he kept going; he was under so much pressure.

Then he got around to me. He said he would like someone with whom he could have lunch occasionally and unload his problems. If he found that person mildly attractive, then he would like to have sex once or twice a month. He said he found me pleasant enough, but he sensed that I couldn't deal with the fact that he was married. (Oh yeah, that's it. It's got nothing to do with the fact that you're carrying more baggage than an American Airlines flight from London. But you think I can't stand that you are married. Let's go with your theory.) I conceded I was bothered by the fact that he was a married man. He understood, and we solemnly parted.

Hope your mother-in-law gives you hell, Carl! ❤

Perry, 40
Engineer
SINGLE

Perry had a very nice voice, and his message was quite detailed. He was obviously proud of his looks as he gave specific details of all his measurements, and I do mean *all*. According to Perry he had great difficulty finding a condom to fit his larger-than-large portion! (Yawn, boring.) Anyway, we agreed to meet at a bookstore where you can sit and drink lattes and act very trendy. I figured that if we had little or nothing in common, then I could at least read a book or two.

I have to admit that Perry *was* very handsome, not too tall but with beautiful eyes and a very nice physique. He ordered me a coffee and got straight to the point.

Perry had answered my ad for one reason only. He wanted sex on a no-strings-attached basis. He would satisfy me, of that he had no doubt whatsoever. In return I would be available to him once or twice a week. We could see other people, of course, and neither of us would ask the other where they had been or why they were out when the other called and all that good stuff. With that off his chest he smiled at me and then looked down at the one that made all his decisions and said, "We've never fucked a real Englishwoman before and we're dying to do it." I asked why he thought my ad meant that I wanted casual sex with someone I hardly knew. He stated with great certainty that "fun times" meant that I wanted sex. If not, I was in breach of advertising standards. Who was he going to report me to, the personal ad police?

As I got up to leave, he said "I could have made you scream, baby." I didn't doubt that. I felt like screaming now and I had only been around him for twenty minutes. I gave him five dollars for my coffee and walked off into the New York sunshine, leaving Perry-Big-Dick to his own devices. ❤

Trevor, 45
Account Manager
MARRIED

Trevor turned up for our date in an ill-fitting suit and cheap sunglasses. He had extremely pale skin with many rough patches that looked like eczema.

He kept his head tilted to the left throughout our date, even when he ate, and I noticed that he licked his lips constantly, though whether they were dry or he was making a lewd gesture for my benefit I don't know.

About halfway through our date a dirty pot of ointment appeared on the table and he massaged the cream into his face. Flakes of skin fell onto the table and into his plate. He looked at me over the top of his sunglasses, which he had not removed, and continued to lick his lips and flake. We had hardly spoken ten words when he suddenly announced, "My penis used to be like my face, but it's okay now. I got some special cream for it." I told Trevor I was happy for him but that I was going home, and I thanked him for meeting me. He became irate and said he wouldn't pay for my food if I was going to behave that way and I should sit down and spend time with him. I glanced at him and his pot of ointment, and walked over to the cashier. As I paid the bill I heard him screwing the lid back on his ointment and surmised that that was the only thing he'll be screwing tonight. ❤

Bill, 40
Plumber
SINGLE

I had difficulty understanding Bill's message on my voicemail as he had a strong New York accent and spoke quickly. I managed to get his number and returned his call. We arranged a meeting for the following evening at a bar in the city, and he told me he would be wearing a beret. He hadn't mentioned that it would be the biggest beret on the biggest head of the biggest neck I had ever seen.

Bill was a very large man who took up almost two seats, and while he may have sported a beret, this guy was no poet. After greeting me with a "How you doin', baby," Bill began to tell me about his work. Okay, he was a plumber, so I didn't expect it to be overly exciting. However, I also didn't expect him to tell me all about the turds he found in customers' toilets. Did you know that most blockages are caused by overlarge, hard turds blocking up the pipes? Furthermore, the holes in the bottoms of toilets are only $1^{1}/_{2}$ inches wide and most men produce turds at least 2 inches in diameter. He spoke about pooh with authority and enthusiasm, making circles with his thumb and forefinger to demonstrate the size.

When he moved on to consistency, I had really had enough. I feigned a headache and told him I had to leave. He wanted to drive me home and became quite insistent. He told me to be careful in New York, as there were some strange people about. Yeah, thanks for your concern, Bill, I would never have guessed. No wonder he was divorced. I can only imagine what he and his ex discussed over their morning bran muffins. ❤

Cess, 29
Mailman
SINGLE

I was a little worried about Cess, who sounded rather unwell when we spoke on the phone—very out of breath and wheezy. Initially I thought he was having sex with the one he loved most, but then I decided he was ill and gave him a chance. He told me he suffered from asthma and other bronchial problems. We arranged to meet at 9:00 A.M. for breakfast in a well-known diner. I don't know why it had to be that early, since he'd already told me he didn't work due to his illness (maybe he had another date after me). At any rate, I got there at nine and he was there, waving to me with one hand and coughing into a handkerchief with the other. Cess had a bad cold to go with his other health woes; his nose was all red and his eyes watery. He smiled at me, said hello, and sneezed all at once. Yuck!

I chatted with the waitress while we ordered—apparently her mother's neighbor had married a man from England, but he was dead now—all the while listening to Cess spluttering and spitting into that handkerchief. I was concerned as to whether he was about to die on me. Perhaps to dispel any notion that his poor health would affect his performance capabilities, Cess grandly announced that he had only one testicle, but the one that he had was more than adequate and I wouldn't be disappointed. Apparently he could do everything that most men with two testicles could, and more. Huh? To cap it off he asked me if I would like to "climb the ladder to success." At this clever witticism he started sniggering, and little bubbles of mucus formed at his nostrils as he told me I wouldn't need a ladder. Oh, how hysterical he was.

When it became clear that he would not be doing the women of the world a favor by expiring on the spot, I took my leave and made my way to another diner, where I sat down to a nice cup of coffee and a decent breakfast. I had not been able to eat with Cess spluttering all over the place. He was one of the most nauseating dates of all. ❤

Matthew, 41
Jeweler
SINGLE

I had to cut this date short because Matthew made me feel sick. What the medical term would be for his condition, I don't know, but in layman's terms, he made grunting piglike noises. It went along the lines of "Hey, glad to meet you ghnughuhgggckckhg. What're you drinking gnguguhhugggukhgkgh." Facial contortions and a shrug of the shoulders accompanied these attractive sounds. On a couple of occasions, he spat into his napkin. Maybe he had a bad cold, sinus problems, or an allergy, but whatever it was, he would have been better off making a date with the pharmacist! ❤

Terry, 38
Lawyer
MARRIED

Poor Terry! His first wife had left him for their neighbor and he had a feeling that wife number two wasn't going to be around for much longer either. She wasn't being very nice to Terry and was exhibiting all the signs of a woman having an affair. Aside from her distinctly icy demeanor, the "fucking bitch" was apparently sucking him dry and not in a sexual way. He would leave her if it weren't for the five kids. (Perhaps he should, before they have six kids.) It was my lucky day, for I was about to hear the entire pathetic story of his crumbling marriage, starting right from the beginning in Ohio up to the present day.

I won't bore you the way Terry bored me, but it did seem that the guy should have worn a sign that read "Hard hats to be worn at all times," just to let females know he was a walking disaster. His marital and financial problems were dire. What I didn't understand was why he was here with me. Wouldn't our date only add to his problems? Had my ad mistakenly given off "I want to be your counselor, come and depress me with your problems" vibes?

He said he needed to speak to someone with no connections to anyone in his family and get their opinion on his problems. Maybe they could be of help, he suggested rather forlornly. I wondered where he had gotten the notion that I could give professional therapy, as it certainly wasn't from me. In fact he didn't want to know anything about me, it was all him, him, him!

I almost cheered when our food arrived, as I felt sure he would have to give my poor little ears a rest while he ate, but no such luck. If anything, he became even more manic, tucking into his food as though it were a race without interrupting his pathetic recitation. Between shoveling and whining, he started to show signs of a nervous tic: Holding his fork in his right hand, he would extend his fingers outward and touch each finger with his thumb. It was nerve-wracking. He'd eaten his entire meal while I had only begun mine. As I ate, he played with his dessert spoon, turning it over and then incorporating it into the finger-touching scenario.

The moment I put my silverware down, Terry said, "Come on, let's go." Upon inquiring just where he wanted me to go, I found out that he had access to a little hotel room where we could go to "let off some steam." Even if my stomach hadn't been churning from my power feeding, I would have found this an unsavory prospect, to put it mildly, and I told him I was tired. He accepted that and we shook hands. Then he ran off.

On the way home I mused that if his sexual performance was on a par with everything else he did, then it's unlikely we would have been in that hotel room for more than a minute or two. Why does Terry have access to a "little hotel room"? Seems to me that he and his wife deserve each other. ❤

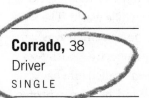

Corrado, 38
Driver
SINGLE

I could hardly understand Corrado's message on the voicemail, and I seriously considered giving him the big D (delete). All I had managed to ascertain was that he was Italian and that he loved soccer. He gave his phone number as if he were five years old!

When I called him, Corrado expressed delight (I think) and asked me to choose a place for our meeting. After repeating it five or six times, he grasped it and that was that.

I fully expected to be stood up, but I was wrong. Corrado turned up only five minutes late. He kissed me on both cheeks in the European manner and sat down opposite me. After just one glass of wine, Corrado told me how much he liked to "mekka lurva." For someone with such rudimentary English, he sure knew how to steer the conversation around to sex in no time flat.

I was wondering how he'd managed to read my ad at all. I knew it was time to go when he took my hand, pointed to a picture on the wall, and said "Look at the lady in the picture, she is very ugly, just like you"! He was smiling at me as though he had paid me a compliment, but I'd had enough. I don't know if he was having a good laugh at my expense, but I wasn't about to stick around to find out.

I thanked him for meeting me, and he asked hopefully, "Where you go, I come, yes?" No, you don't, Corrado.

I got the check and shook his hand as I made to leave. He asked, "You don't mekka lurva to Corrado, no?"

No, I go mekka dinner for me. *Ciao,* Corrado. ❤

Latrell (in his dreams), 30
Pro Basketball Player
(in his best-ever dreams)
SINGLE

This guy must be the unluckiest liar in the whole world. The message on the voicemail was very hey-baby-smoochy-woochy-sexy sexy. When I called him back, he told me his name was Latrell Sprewell and he was a professional basketball player with the New York Knicks. He went on to explain that we should get together as soon as possible as the Knicks were going on the road in a few days. I was barely able to set a date for lunch before I put the phone down and burst out laughing. This guy would have me believe he was a million-dollar basketball player. If he had gone for a football or baseball player, I would have probably been taken in. But just his luck, my son, Daniel, attends an American high school on a basketball scholarship, and his favorite player is Allen Houston who plays for . . . the New York Knicks. So I was actually quite clued up on Mr. Sprewell and company. This was going to be an interesting date.

"Latrell" was sitting at the bar when I arrived, and seated he was taller than most of the guys standing. All right, he was the correct height for a hoopster. (See, I know the lingo.) He was also very good looking. So I sat with him at the bar and he was looking very cool and wasn't fazed when I asked him where he was playing next. I had already checked, and I knew it was the Orlando Magic. He knew that too and said the Magic would be no problem for him. We ordered wine and some appetizers. Then he (I refuse to call him Latrell) asked questions about me, and reacted calmly when I told him about my son and how I just loved basketball. I went on and on and ended with "Could you get Allen Houston's autograph for my son?" Unfortunately he couldn't, as Allen didn't like to sign autographs. What a surprise! I asked if I could come and see him play, and that was big fat *no* as well. I had to ask why a man in his position would answer a personal ad, and wasn't I a little old for him. He countered that "always being on the road got lonely," blah blah blah, and he liked older women.

I must have been asking too many questions because he cut the date short by telling me he had received a phone call while in the men's room and had to leave. How he accomplished that trick with his cell phone in his jacket, which was slung over the back of the barstool, is anyone's guess. He kissed me good-bye and promised to call when he could.

Once he'd left, I asked the bartender if he knew the guy I had been with, and he said he'd seen him in the place before but had no idea who he was. Maybe it was the wine, but I felt the need to share the fact that he'd told me he was Latrell Sprewell. The bartender went into convulsions of laughter and told some other guys at the other end of the bar, who yelled out, "Hey, sweetheart, come and sit on my lap—I'm Donald Trump" and "I'll buy you dinner—I'm Michael Jordan" amid guffaws of laughter. Even I had to laugh at the Jordan crack, as the guy who made it was short and white. Not surprisingly, I never heard from "Latrell" again. All he wanted was someone he could spin a line to and along came me, Little Miss NBA. What's funny is that whenever I see the Knicks play, I feel like I know Latrell. ❤

Lou, 33
Firefighter
SINGLE

Lou wanted to take me to a very fancy restaurant for lobster—that was his favorite! (So why would he assume that it was my favorite too? He certainly didn't ask.)

The restaurant he'd chosen *was* extremely nice, and when I arrived, I was shown to the table where Lou was waiting. He was a sight for sore eyes: nice looking, with a tan and quite fit from what I could see. When he stood to greet me, however, I noticed that he was wearing the tightest pants I'd ever seen. All his "private bits and pieces" seemed to have been scooped together and held captive in a manner that looked uncomfortable to say the least.

At Lou's urging I ordered the lobster tail with a steak. As we waited for the food, I asked why he had answered my ad, and he told me he'd had a longtime girlfriend with whom he'd parted badly. When he was at work one day, she called him to say she was going shopping. What she failed to tell him was that she was going shopping at his apartment! When he came home the place was completely empty, making him feel, he said, just like Mother Hubbard.

I thought that was a strange way for a grown man to characterize his home having been looted, but I let it pass.

Because of that incident, Lou went on, he wasn't going to settle down again—hence his reply to my ad. He just wanted to "hang loose like Jack from the beanstalk." I started to laugh at this second fairy tale allusion, but Lou ordered a bottle of wine and we spoke about his job, which he enjoyed very much. Suddenly he fell silent and looked off into the distance. I saw his eyes fill with tears. Alarmed, I asked if he was okay, to which he replied, "I'm just thinking about *Bambi*. The first time I saw it I cried, and when I watched it today, I cried again."

Thankfully our food arrived and Lou regained his (relative) good spirits.

Over our meal—which was, by the way, delicious—he asked, "Do you think I resemble Peter Pan? People have said that I do." He didn't wait for my answer, but mused aloud that he wished he could fly just like Peter Pan, that he would give Michael Jordan a run for his money! At that he laughed, saying that he had made a "funny." We ate the rest of the meal in silence. He was probably replaying fairy tales in his head, while I was wondering how these nursery rhyme fantasies jibed with his anatomically correct trousers.

Lou said he had an early start the next day and called for the check. He also said he would take me home and became agitated when I told him I had my car outside. "You're not going home alone," he said. "Look what happened to Red Riding Hood!" I burst out laughing then, unable to contain myself any longer. He looked aghast and asked how I could be so callous and uncaring.

I had no idea what he was going on about, but I knew I had to get away. As he stood to leave, he said, "This is America, baby. There are some very strange people out there, and you need to be more concerned."

I was concerned that the zipper on his pants would rip and we would see his winkle.

As we walked to our respective cars, I saw Lou across the street, performing ballerina-type arabesques. Did that man tell me he was a firefighter?

As he kindly mentioned, there are some strange people out there. ❤

Leo, 27
Therapist
SINGLE

Leo and I met at a hotel on the beach, which he explained would be convenient for him because his office was located in one of the hotel units. It was a hot day, and he asked if it was okay if we sat outside. I agreed with that because if the meeting didn't go well, at least I could get a bit of a suntan.

Leo was of medium height and weight, with sandy blond hair he wore swept back. He asked what I would like to drink, and even before it arrived, he launched into a litany of his problems and woes. His eyes filled with tears, he bit his upper lip, then he took a deep breath and said, "I feel as though my life is in ruins." Apparently his girlfriend of five years had left him for one of his good friends. He felt betrayed by both of them and was at times suicidal. Had I ever felt so low myself, he asked.

I was about to murmur a sympathetic response when suddenly he jumped up and said, "Oh I love this song, whooh yeah." It was Mariah Carey's "Dream Lover," and he really did seem to love it. He clamped his feet and knees together and moved his shoulders up and down in spasmodic movements, indicating with a jerk of his head for me to join him on the dance floor. (There was no dance floor!) The moment the song ended, he returned to his seat and picked up his tearjerker story without missing a beat, to a now far less sympathetic ear. After all, how suicidal can you be when a Mariah Carey song is all it takes to elevate your mood?

The conversation turned to his work and how he didn't really like animals at all. In fact, he confided, he didn't know why he bothered—life isn't really all it's cracked up to be, is it? Again, he didn't wait for my answer. He heard Dr. Dre and was off, those knees and feet locked together and the shoulders doing their stuff. "C'mon," he urged, "it's Dre." I know Dre is a doctor but surely no song can have such restorative powers. This man was a fraud, and I didn't want to stay there and be his unpaid counselor and occasional dance partner. I told him I really had to get going, which led him to ask plaintively why everyone had to leave him. I was considering telling him the truth, but then he jumped up and started his little ritual all over again, this time to Snoop Doggy Dog. I wanted to laugh as he spun around, singing along with his new favorite tune. Yes, he'd added a spin to his repertoire. It was a sight to behold. I called out good-bye and he incorporated a wave into the increasingly elaborate dance routine. I decided he was definitely better off with the animals, but were the animals better off with him? ❤

Tony, 26
Waiter
SINGLE

Tony lied about his age and about his occupation. He had answered my ad hoping to find a woman who would buy him gifts and help him out with cash. In reality, he confessed, he was a twenty-year-old college student who worked only part-time as a waiter—in fact only on Saturdays.

He also told me he wasn't hungry, which I belatedly realized was more a reflection of his wallet than his stomach, as he picked food off my plate while I was eating.

As he watched me eat, Tony said he liked me and he knew that he could please me for hours on end. I told him that right now, I would be very pleased if he just stopped taking my food with his fingers. If he was hungry, then I would pay for his food, but he needed to stop fondling mine! He promptly ordered a pizza with more toppings than they had, and a glass of wine that he wasn't old enough to be drinking.

I was ready to bring this sad meeting to a conclusion when Tony said, "If you give me some money each week, I'll give you the best sex you've ever had." He added, "I know I'm good in bed because I had sex with a girl at school who has really slept around and she said I was the best."

Ah, youth. That "you're the best" line is the oldest trick in the book. That girl from college had got her act together!

As I was leaving, Tony said, "Have you got any friends I can meet then, one not as old as you?"

I didn't think that question deserved an answer. ❤

Steven, 41
Entrepreneur
SINGLE

This man told me his entire life story within minutes of our meeting. His family, he said, had been extremely poor and he had gone without a lot of the things that kids need and he had never got over it. Now he had money, which I guess explains why he was wearing so much jewelry. The rap stars on MTV would have been jealous of the collection of gold chains around his neck.

Of course we had our date in a very fancy restaurant that Steven knew, and he of course ordered expensive wine after I refused Champagne. Although he was now quite wealthy he could not find a woman to love or to love him, he said. There was nothing wrong with Steven's looks, but as he spoke, it became clear there was something wrong with his personality, or at least the way he went about his dates. He went straight for the sympathy vote, wanting me to feel sorry for him because of his deprived childhood and craving praise for his achievements. Every time he opened his mouth an even sadder story came out: He never had a bike. He used to look out of the window at the other kids on their roller skates. Well, sorry and all that, but you are over forty, for God's sake—get over it! There aren't too many women I know who like a whingy wimpy man who wants constant praise. He told me he didn't have many dates; women were put off by him. No kidding! Take some of those bloody chains off for a start, and stop wallowing in self-pity. Not once did he ask about me; he only wanted to talk about himself. A big no-no on a first date, right?

I got to wondering if this man was lying about all this childhood poverty just to gain my sympathy. Either way, it wasn't working; his miserable ways were a real turn-off. I seized the opportunity to tell him I was really doing research for a book. How would he feel about that? Far from being angry, he was impressed, and asked me to tell the women of New York that a single, very wealthy, and nice-looking man is ready to meet them!

Ladies, two out of three ain't bad. If anyone does want to contact him, they can write to the publisher and I guess we can put you in touch. It's all part of the service. But be prepared to do a lot of sympathetic shoulder patting. ❤

Joey, 31
Artist
SINGLE

"I'm sexy, fit, and Italian" was Joey's message on my voicemail. "If you call me, then you'll never call another man again!"

Now, that could be taken two ways, couldn't it?

As it turned out, Joey *was* nice to look at. He could also be described as sexy, but since that's such a subjective evaluation, shouldn't someone *else* make that statement about *you*?

We ordered a drink, and while we were waiting, Joey offered that the last Englishwoman he had met was so hot in bed that she wore him out! He went on to tell me how sensitive he was in bed, and how passionate and pleasing he was to a woman. He wanted me to know that he could and would "take me to the height of passion and bring me back down."

As he spoke, he began to lick the outside of his wineglass, looking very silly indeed. In fact he was getting quite steamed up all by himself, and it wasn't a pretty sight. If he thought he was turning me on, he was so wrong. I was desperately trying not to laugh, but it was impossible. I gave in to the pains I was getting in my side and burst out laughing.

Joey immediately stopped his performance and said he was leaving—he wasn't staying to be ridiculed. I nodded and accepted his departure with grace. As he walked away, he shook his head and announced that I would be forever sorry.

Didn't anyone ever let him know that self-praise is no recommendation? ❤

Maurice, 36
Office Manager
SINGLE

Maurice wasted no time in telling me that he was a real man. He said he had broad shoulders and a strong jaw, he liked to treat a woman well, and he had no problem meeting females; he was just giving the personals a try. We arranged to meet for dinner at seven the following evening.

Maurice was very nice looking, and he paid me some nice compliments too, but only ten minutes into our date he took the conversation south. He was a very good lover, he said, but he wanted me to know that he snored! I asked why he felt I needed to know this, to which he replied, looking confused, "Well, I like you, and I know you like me, so aren't we going to get it on?" When I indicated the date was officially over, he asked if I was upset because he had told me he snored. If that was the case, he assured me, "You can go after we've done it."

After? No thanks, Maurice. I think I'll go now! ❤

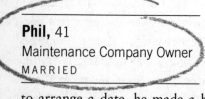

Phil, 41
Maintenance Company Owner
MARRIED

Phil worked hard to create the impression that he was so busy he hardly had time to breathe. When he called to arrange a date, he made a huge deal of not being able to make the time I suggested, saying "Whoa, no, just can't do it, uh uh no, can't manage it." Then he said, "How about seven forty-five?" I agreed that seven forty-five would be a fine time to meet, as it was only fifteen minutes later than my original suggestion.

When we met up, Phil waved to me from a table in the center of the room. The other hand was holding some kind of walkie-talkie, which was making loud noises. At the end of every message, there would be a loud hissing and crackling combined with a "diddle ooh diddle ooh." Annoying, to say the least.

With his free hand, Phil pulled out a chair and motioned for me to sit. The same hand made a "Do you want a drink?" movement, then a gesture to the waiter. All the while, he was still speaking into the walkie-talkie. When the waiter arrived, Phil pointed at me and I ordered a glass of wine. Phil then pointed at his own empty glass, looked at the waiter, and nodded, raising his eyebrows. He was still talking, though not to me. When our drinks arrived, we clinked our glasses together in a silent "cheers." Looking at the menu, Phil pointed to the buffalo wings, then put his fingers to his lips and squinted his eyes in what I took to be his way of communicating that they were good. Then he fanned his hand in front of his mouth, letting me know that the wings were very hot!

Eventually Phil ended his conversation and began to tell me all the wonderful functions of his new gadget. For those who care (and I wasn't one of them), this was a cell phone *and* a walkie-talkie that allowed him to talk to his "fleet" for free while using the "CB" part of the phone, thereby saving lots of money in cell phone charges. Phil obviously loved his new toy, since we spoke about nothing else whatsoever. And when he wasn't talking about its wonders, he was using the phone to contact his "fleet."

After an hour or so, I pretended to receive a call on my own cell phone. When I said I had to leave, Phil took one look at my phone and shook his head, disparaging its make and paucity of functions. The man was a walking advertisement for Nextel phones! He was also a walking advertisement for boredom. ❤

Tom-Tim, 40
Management Consultant
SINGLE

"Hello, my name is Tom-Tim and I am your girly-boy." That is the message I received from this particular caller. What the hell is a "girly-boy," I asked myself, and what kind of a name is Tom-Tim? In the good name of research, I called him back at the number he'd left, and he answered, "This is Tom-Tim." I explained who I was but he seemed not to recall having left me a message, asking me to hold the line for a second. When he came back on, his manner had done a complete turnaround. Somebody had been in his office a few moments earlier and he hadn't been able to talk freely. We quickly arranged to meet up the following day for lunch, and I told him I was looking forward to it. In truth I *was* looking forward to finding out what this "girly-boy" business was all about.

Tom-Tim had chosen a Chinese restaurant for our rendezvous, and he was there when I arrived; he looked completely normal. Immediately, however, he started to act like a six-year-old brat. It was so comical. He asked me if he could have some wine and started pouting and squealing, albeit very quietly. He kicked his legs about under the table and fidgeted on his seat. I couldn't stop laughing at his antics, which seemed to make him angry. He asked me not to laugh, as people were looking at me. At *me*! They couldn't possibly be looking at you, wiggling about and screwing your face up like some kind of maniac, could they? Despite my bouts of giggles, Tom-Tim pressed on, explaining he wanted me to act like his mother and tell him off, all while he behaved like an ill-mannered toddler.

After about half an hour of his nonsense, he gave up and said that he could see I wasn't really into this. (You got that right!) When he suggested we shouldn't meet up again, I agreed wholeheartedly. He paid the bill and asked if I would allow him to leave first, as he didn't want *me* to follow *him*! No problem. I sat and finished my food and started to laugh at the recollection of his antics. Now people *were* looking at me! ❤

Paul, 35
Mechanic (AAA)
MARRIED

Paul spoke very quietly when he left his message, and he sounded nervous, as if he was worried about being overheard. He said he was "kinda" married and that he liked women "who had teddy bears" on their bed. I found out what he really meant by that statement when we met.

The event took place at an all-you-can-eat buffet. Paul was waiting for me in the foyer, uniform on, so he was easy to spot. He stood around five nine, with a stocky build and light brown hair. He had already put our name on the list, and as we were waiting to be seated I tried to make conversation, but Paul asked if we could wait to talk when we were seated. He didn't speak again, so I became engrossed in the hostess and the way she assigned diners to their tables. She reminded me of the bailiff on *Judge Judy:* "Jones, party of three, step forward please." Like we were being punished, not having a meal. (Maybe she knew something we didn't!) Eventually Paul's name was called and we "stepped forward" to our table. Immediately Paul went off to get food. By the looks of his plate, he had gathered enough to feed the party of six waiting to step forward!

He suggested I go and get my food as there was a helluva

lot of good stuff there and he only had forty-five minutes to spend with me. (Oh God, that long?) As I returned to the table, Paul was off, getting his second plate.

When he got back, I tried again to start a conversation by asking why he had answered my ad. Through mouthfuls of pasta (he didn't stop eating), he told me that he was trying to find someone special. Then he did pause, just for a second or two, and asked, "Do you like playing with your teddy bears? I mean, *really* playing with your teddy bears?" Warming to his subject now, he actually laid down his fork as he said, "I love to watch a woman get physical with a stuffed animal—it really turns me on," adding a special wink for me. With that he headed back to the buffet.

He returned to the table with chocolate cake, but said he was going to the car and would be right back. I briefly hoped he might be taking off, but I knew he wouldn't leave without his cake. When he returned he handed me a shopping bag. Inside was a teddy bear. Proudly, through mouthfuls of chocolate cake, Paul told me the bear could be mine if I wanted it!

I didn't, and I told him so, but he apparently misunderstood my refusal, for he asked if I would have preferred a stuffed pig instead. I looked at his chocolate-crumbed lips, and it was all I could do to stop myself from saying, "No, thank you, I've just had one." Instead I just said that I thought we wanted different things and we shouldn't meet up again. As I left, he turned around in his seat to call after me, "A snake, then—what about a stuffed snake?" I didn't bother to answer. As I approached the exit the bailiff bellowed, "Keep to the left please, to the left."

On the way home, I wondered what could have possibly happened in Paul's life to make him excited by stuffed toys. Wow, men! Just when you think you've heard it all. I wonder how many times that teddy has been offered around. Come to think of it, I don't want to know. ❤

Mark, 45
Locksmith
SINGLE

Mark liked my ad and said he "just couldn't wait" to meet me. After a very brief "how will we recognize each other" phone call, we arranged a date.

I looked out for the "forty-five-year-old, five-foot-seven, brown-haired, athletic-looking man" with no luck. But he saw me, and came over to say hello. I couldn't help thinking that if Mark had been a little more specific in his description, then I would have had no trouble picking him out. But he chose to omit the very important fact that he would be wearing a skirt! Not only that, but also a blouse, women's boots, and badly applied makeup!

He looked ridiculous. In fact the only nice thing about his appearance was the wig he was wearing. I decided to make the best of it and asked what was going on here. Apparently this was Mark's way of relaxing and unwinding. (Whatever happened to kicking off your shoes and relaxing on the couch with glass of wine?) He realized he needed some help with the makeup. He wondered if I could help. Or maybe we could go out as "girlfriends."

No, we couldn't. I finished my drink and told Mark that I had to leave but it had been very nice to meet. I paid our check and watched as Mark sashayed into the ladies' room. I wanted to get out of there, pronto. When they found out that Mark was not all he should be, there would be some very cross women in that room . . . perfect for a cross-dresser. ❤

James, 37
Care Assistant
SINGLE

When I heard James's message, I wanted to laugh. There was music playing in the background and he was speaking in a very odd way, peppering his lines with "and um." The message he left went along the lines of "Heard your ad, and um, I like the sound of you, and um, I like playing video games and um writing poetry and um legs in black stockings." The last gave me pause, but how bad could he be? Look at the wide range of interests this man had.

We met up for a drink at a German Bierkeller, where James ordered a beer for himself "and um" a Diet Coke for me. He was five feet eight, with a nice round face and red cheeks like an apple.

Straight away, James launched into that day's activities. He was off work, so he got up late and um, went to the laundromat. Then he went to the store and um got some food while the clothes were washing. I tried to feign interest, but his recitation was incredibly boring. I kept myself awake by counting the number of times he said "and um." When I got to sixteen and he still had his washing in the dryer, I knew I needed an escape plan. I couldn't think of one, so I just came out and told him I had to leave. He continued on, as if I hadn't spoken. "I brought my Game Boy to the laundromat, and um I played it until the clothes were done, and um I went to a friend's house, and um had a beer, and um and um and um." What was this guy all about? I picked up my bag, and said good-bye to James. He said, "Okay, see you around, and um I'll call you." With that, he turned around and began speaking to two unsuspecting women. All I heard was "I didn't go to work today, and um." I knew the rest. So I headed for the door, and um hailed a cab and um went home! ❤

Craig, 44
Cab Driver
SINGLE

Craig presented himself well on the phone, but our date was one of the worst. When I arrived at the Spanish restaurant he had chosen, he was already at the table. He stood to greet me and as he put his hand out, I noticed many scabs up his arm. His dark hair was unkempt and his green eyes were bloodshot. Overall he had a wild, unhealthy appearance.

He ordered a drink for me and a double for himself, then told me, "I used to be a famous football player." I had to believe him—what do I know about American football? I said, "Oh, what part did you play?" Craig answered with "It's not the theater. I was a running back."

Before I could say anything more, Craig leaned forward and said, "My luck has been so bad since I started doing drugs, I've reached rock bottom." He continued on. "I feel like dying tonight. Wanna come with me?"

That was my cue to "wanna" get right out of there.

Craig took out the newspaper where he had seen my ad and tore a scrap off. Then he reached into his sock for his drugs and was about to put some in the paper for me before I told him firmly that I didn't want any drugs. He told me I needed to "shoot something up my nose" to fully understand him, and anyway, I was an "uptight bitch."

That may be so, but this uptight bitch was going home. When he went to the men's room to do his "thing," I left.

The way Craig was carrying on, his wish about dying may well come true. After our date I asked around about him, and a few people actually did know his name. Fame and glory are indeed fleeting, and it takes a stronger man than Craig to thrive outside the limelight. ❤

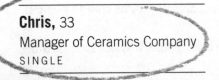

Chris, 33
Manager of Ceramics Company
SINGLE

Chris had a big, booming voice that made me jump when his message came on. I spilt my coffee! We had a chat—a *loud* chat—and decided on a meeting the following evening. Chris wanted me to come to his home at first, but he understood when I refused and we settled on an Italian place he knew.

Turned out Chris craved attention . . . and not only when he spoke.

Over seafood linguine, Chris told me in a booming voice that he really loved to be watched as he masturbated, which he would like to do later! I would be required to "watch and watch only." He said, "What d'you say?" When I said, "Thanks, but no thanks," he wasn't fazed at all. He leaned forward and asked me, "Did I tell you I had nine and a half inches?"

I would have been embarrassed even if he weren't broadcasting the size of his willy to everyone in the restaurant. As it was I felt positively mortified.

I couldn't finish my food. I told Chris I had to get going. He said, "Okay babe. You call me if you change your mind, now." When I offered to get the check, he wouldn't hear of it. He winked at me, saying, "No problem. I know you'll be calling me before the week's out. The next one's on you." I had a pretty good idea what the "next one" might be, and I certainly didn't want it "on me." ❤

Terry, 41
Hotel Manager
SINGLE

Priapism. I had never run across that particular condition before I met Terry. But he felt I should know from the top that he had a hard-on all the time. Apparently his penis was "standing at attention" even as we spoke. Should I be flattered, angry? No, he couldn't help it, it was just there!

I didn't know whether to believe him. It was a strange thing to tell someone on a first date. We were only having a drink, after all. Come to think of it, if we were going to take it that step further and have sex, his penis would presumably have "risen to the occasion" and there would be no reason to inform me of his "never-ending erection." I would just have been very pleasantly surprised! So I decided he was lying. What a complete jerk! A grown man, telling a relative stranger about his penis!

When he had stopped talking about his penis, he spoke about his job in the hotel. He had been the manager for four years and he loved it. However, because of the hours he worked, he didn't get a chance to socialize and meet women. That was why he had answered my ad. Terry was quite good looking. He stood about six feet and had a nice physique. There was a gym at the hotel and he used it every day. He also ran in marathons, and he liked to go salsa dancing.

He told me that he found me attractive and would like to see me again—there would always be a place for me at his hotel. I thanked him very much, but said that as it was getting late, I really had to go. He was standing up now, and I couldn't help looking down in the general direction of his condition. (Oh come on, you would have too.) There did seem to be quite a bulge, and his pants weren't especially tight either. I put my hand out to shake his, and he pulled me towards him, saying, "Give me a hug." I quickly shoved my handbag between us (sorry, Louis Vuitton), then pulled away and began walking to the exit. He came running over and whispered, "I can't get condoms to fit. Will that be okay with you?" Whatever, Terry!

Was he telling the truth about the "other thing"? I wasn't about to find out. Still, maybe he can get his condoms made to measure. Or check out those "big, tall man" stores. Surely they sell "personal" products in "small, medium, and liar"! ❤

Derek, 37
Lawyer
SINGLE

Derek told me he looked like a television star, and he did: He was the spitting image of George Costanza from *Seinfeld*. He had assumed that I wouldn't know who George was; he was amazed that I knew the show at all. Know it? I love it! I was there with the rest of the world for the final episode.

Anyway, we had a drink together and Derek asked if I liked wrestling. I told him that my son liked the WWF at one time; I had even taken him to a "summer slam" or some such nonsense.

No, no. Derek said he liked to watch *women* wrestle. In fact, he liked to watch them wrestle in the nude. He was a member of a club that held wrestling contests every Friday. He asked if I would like to accompany him on his next visit. Why would I want to watch female wrestlers, and naked ones at that? Apparently I had misunderstood his question. He wanted me to *participate* in the Friday night competition, not just watch! The winner took home a hundred dollars and all she could drink, he assured me. "How about it?" he asked.

When I said I wasn't about to get my kit off in a seedy bar, get half killed by raunchy Rhonda, and show all my stuff to the male patrons just to win a hundred bucks, Derek got upset with me. Apparently I had no get-up-and-go! Oh really? Watch this, Derek. ❤

Tommy, 55
Furniture Upholsterer
SINGLE

When a fifty-five-year-old man says he's never been married, you usually don't have to wait long to discover the reason.

Tommy told me that he had dated quite a few women from the personal ads, but that I was the first Englishwoman he had ever spoken to in real life and he was very excited to be meeting me. He went on to tell me that he hadn't found a lasting relationship either through the ads or in everyday meetings with women, and he thought that maybe he was too choosy. And anyway, he said, he enjoyed the single man's life.

Tommy had suggested a Japanese steakhouse, where they cook in front of you and "do all kinds of stuff and tricks" with the food. When I got to the restaurant, he was at the bar eating all the free snacks and drinking a beer. He suggested that I didn't really need to get a drink now, as we would be going to the table in a minute or two. I was beginning to see why Tommy had difficulty sustaining a relationship.

He was an ordinary-looking man, a little overweight and wearing a jacket that was way too tight. He noted my suntan and asked if I had been on vacation. But as soon as I began to reply, he started talking about the wall coverings and how ugly they were. When I tried to speak again, he put his finger over my lips, saying, "Just like a woman, yap yap yap." This was one rude man.

We were seated opposite the chef at a table for ten people. As the chef introduced himself and went around the table asking everybody's name, Tommy yelled out, "Come on, One Hung Low, just get on with it, will ya? Some of us are hungry." Then he searched around the table looking for support and began laughing loudly and clapping his hands. I felt like hiding under the table.

The chef continued on with his patter and took our food orders. When it came to Tommy's turn, he said "Bring it on, Ching Chong."

It only got worse. As our soup was brought to the table, a man at the end refused his. Tommy heard and asked for it, saying to me, "You have it—you're a skinny thing." He wouldn't listen to my protests and poured the soup into my bowl! By this time I had taken all I could, and I don't mean soup. I asked where the ladies' room was. I did go in there, but of course it was at the other end of the restaurant, well away from the front door. I was determined not to go back to Tommy. I needed to sneak out without him seeing me. I really shouldn't have worried, though, or flattered myself that he would care. As I made my way back towards the table, Tommy, oblivious to everything, was jostling for space beside the chef, who was asking him to please take his seat. I saw that Tommy was elbowing him, trying to get hold of the knives. The chef was yelling out in Japanese, probably asking the manager to call 911. That's all I needed. I kept on walking, right out the door, followed by the manager, who told me to "take that with you" and pointed at Tommy, who was making unattractive gestures with his face and fingers.

No, thanks. I'll pass.

Come to think of it, it's a good thing Tommy enjoys being single. There can't be too many women lining up for a date with him. ❤

Darryl, 44
Dentist
SINGLE

Darryl suggested we meet at a beach bar for lunch. I was a little concerned about wearing swimwear on a date with a stranger, so I decided on a one-piece bathing suit with a wrap, and felt as though I looked quite decent. Our telephone conversation had been brief but very upbeat on Darryl's part. He was "living life to the full, babe, 'cos you're a long time dead, man." He had told me to "get my butt over here and let's party, Mama."

As it turned out, it was Darryl's butt that made an appearance. When he walked up to me, I noticed that Darryl's swimsuit was small, but I didn't realize it was a thong until he led the way to our table. The man must have weighed three hundred pounds. As he sprawled in his chair, Darryl drank Jack Daniels and told me about his two ex-wives. Both of them were "fucking neurotic bitches" who hadn't given him any children. He ordered "another John Daniels," adding, "When you know him as well as I do, you can call him anything you want," and started to fiddle with the front of his swimsuit while telling me he wished he had a son. I, on the other hand, had already had too much sun, and when he ordered another drink, I stood up to go. Darryl kissed me on both cheeks (no, I wasn't wearing a thong too) and said he knew I'd had a great time, as he was such a fun guy! ❤

men with something extra

Mother always said it was rude to arrive at someone's home empty-handed, but I don't think the same can be said for a date. In fact, given what these fellows had up their sleeves, the opposite may hold true. For reasons known only to themselves, each of the men in this chapter felt the need to bring something—or someone—along with him. Whether gifts, props, moral support, or reinforcements, the "something extra" each of them brought to the table certainly set the tone for our date. Sure, it might be nice to bring flowers to a blind date, but underwear? I mean *really*.

I didn't accept any presents from the dates who came bearing gifts; there wasn't one of them that I felt like being beholden to. Read on and you'll see why.

Apparently Quin's father had the contract for cleaning a certain stretch of the ocean beachfront. He owned three large tractor-type vehicles that scooped up all the garbage left by visitors. When his father died, Quin would inherit this lucrative business, he claimed. Quin was quite a nice guy when he stopped speaking about the imminent death of his dad!

I asked if his father was sick, and he said, "Oh no. I just wanted you to know that when he dies, all three tractors will be mine." We were at a beach restaurant where everybody seemed to know Quin. I guessed it was his local hangout.

Despite his rather morbid opening line, Quin was rather charming. The food was delicious and I began to relax. Over a glass of wine, I asked Quin why he had answered my ad, and he said that he was looking for some hot sex. He didn't bat an eyelid as he said that.

Before I had a chance to react to this matter-of-fact statement, along came dear old dad. Quin introduced me as his English girlfriend. His father was very pleasant and sat down to join us, but when Quin went to the men's room, he asked if his son had treated me like a lady. I gathered from his question that Quin had some problems where women were concerned. As fast as he could, before Quin returned, he told me that his son had the unfortunate habit of exposing himself to members of the opposite sex!

Even quicker, I told Quin's father that I was leaving. He nodded his head as if he fully expected and understood my reaction, even pointing the way to the back exit. I jumped into my car and headed home, not quite sure what to make of this strange twosome.

Later, I reflected that if Quin's father really was so wealthy from his beach cleaning service, perhaps he should spend some of that money on therapy for his wayward son. ❤

Randy, 48
Gun Shop Owner
SINGLE

No, he didn't bring me a Smith & Wesson special, but he did bring his mother and she was no prize!

Randy explained that Mom didn't like to be alone and that the woman who was to have stayed with her had had a fire in her trailer.

Randy was very tall—six feet four, he said—and his mother was very tall too. It's really unusual to see elderly women who are tall, but this one must have been almost six feet. She wouldn't speak to me, and Randy had to tell her to "be nice now!" I tried to "be nice now" too, but after getting no response to the three questions I asked, I gave up. She did, however, speak to her son as if I weren't there.

When Randy and I tried to talk, Mom butted in and spoke to Randy about trivial stuff. She was clearly jealous, but she had no need to worry—her son was no prize either! When he wasn't discussing some mundane thing with his mother, he spoke almost continuously about certain legislators who were campaigning for gun control and what he'd like to do to them. I decided to keep my opinions to myself as he ranted on that everybody had the right to bear arms. Why, even his mother had a gun to protect herself, he told me. She was looking at me as if she'd like to put her weapon to use that very minute, and I couldn't help noticing how her hands shook as she spooned her soup into her mouth. She has a gun? I'm certain that if she were to shoot at someone, twenty-three innocent bystanders would go down. Still, I kept quiet. What else could I do? The old lady was packing, right?

Randy also swore a lot. It was effing this and effing that, and everyone he mentioned was either a motherfucker or an asshole! All this bad language in front of his own mother, too!

I was ready to call it quits, but wouldn't you know it, Randy had to go to the bathroom. Mom and I didn't exchange a word the whole time he was gone, despite his insistence that she tell me about the family. She sucked on her dentures and I chewed my lip. As soon as he returned, I told him I had to go and offered to split the bill. He put his arm around me and hugged me, telling me I was a "sweetie pie" and he had no intention of taking my money. He also informed me that next time, we would do something a little special, just the two of us (or three, if you counted the gun he was no doubt carrying). I didn't dare look at Ma Barker! The moment he paid the bill, Randy's mother got up, linked her arm through his, and stood there, stony-faced. I said good-bye and retreated into the bathroom until I was sure they had left.

Randy was quite unpleasant on his own, but as a double feature, they were the worst ever. No wonder he is still single at the age of forty-eight! ❤

Mark, 37
Real Estate Broker
SINGLE

Mark told me he looked like Kenny Rogers, but to me, he looked more like one of Kenny Rogers's roasters! He had been to Jamaica the week before and had gotten very badly sunburned. His face and ears were red and peeling, and I couldn't resist asking why he hadn't cancelled our date until he felt (and looked?) better. The man was positively glowing and he was giving off more heat than an oven!

Anyway, Mark and I had a drink at a hotel bar; he had suggested that if we got on we would have dinner. Apparently the date was going better from his side than mine, as he passed me a large blue box, beaming. Inside were a handbag and a wallet from a famous designer. Or so I thought! "It's fake," Mark exclaimed proudly. "Isn't it authentic? It's yours." Actually, it really did look good, but there was no way I could accept it. So

I thanked him for the thought, but declined the gifts. He looked crestfallen and the evening went downhill from that point.

When Mark began picking his peeling ears, it was time for me to leave. He shook my hand, and with his free hand he continued to peel the tip of his ear. I thanked him for meeting me and we went our separate ways. I watched as he, the blue box, and his red face made for the door. ❤

Carl, 44
Office Furniture Company Owner
MARRIED

Carl asked if we could meet for lunch at a hotel where he had a morning meeting, and I agreed. He told me how he would be dressed so I would know how to recognize him: "I'll be wearing a beige cashmere, darling!"

Carl wasn't there when I arrived, and I anxiously glanced at my watch as I sat at the table he had booked. It's always a nervous time when you are waiting for a date to show. He turned up after just a few minutes, laden with shopping bags and explaining that as his meeting had ended a little early, he had decided to do a bit of shopping before our date. Once we were served our drinks, he leaned down to rummage around in his shopping bags and handed me a bag from a well-known lingerie store. "I got most of the stuff in average size, but I guessed on the bra size. I buy all my girlfriends underwear."

I was really uncomfortable with the thought of this man purchasing my intimate apparel. It was creepy! "I know that you Brits call panties 'knickers,' so I got you some," he said, smiling now. He urged me to take them out of the bag and look at them, and then he leaned over and said, "Go and put a pair on and let me see." What? I already had "knickers" on, thank you very much, and Carl would not be seeing them! But he wouldn't stop. He tried coaxing, "Oh go on, baby, try them on." He turned to flattery. "You are so sexy—they will look great on you." Finally he said, "Don't be a bitch. Just put them on." Oh yes, Carl that will do it every time.

I took the bag into the bathroom and asked the hostess to return it to "the man in the beige cashmere," and I hit the road. I hope Carl had the forethought to buy "one size fits all," because this Brit wasn't in the habit of taking candy, or knickers, from a stranger! ❤

Wayne, 40
Auto Dealership Owner
SINGLE

Wayne brought a friend along on our date, which made me very uncomfortable. When the friend went to the bathroom, Wayne apologized for having him there, explaining that he had been unable to shake him off. I didn't believe him for a second. How difficult could it be to tell your friend that you have a date and will catch up with him later?

It got better. When Wayne went to the bathroom, his friend instantly started bad-mouthing him, warning me that he beat up his last girlfriend and that I should be careful! I wasn't sure whether to believe him, either, but I didn't want to take any chances, and I was outnumbered. Since we were taking turns visiting the bathrooms, I excused myself and just kept on walking.

I've never liked threesomes (as previous relationships will testify), and this was no exception. ❤

Ted, 40
Trader
SINGLE

Ted was a nice-looking man, all pin-stripe-suited and booted. He carried a battered briefcase in one hand and in the other a large table lamp. He set the lamp down on the floor and shook my hand. As he sat down, he asked how I liked the lamp. It was actually quite ugly, a bright green chalk-type base with a darker green shade. But out of politeness I said that it was nice, to which he said, "Good, I bought it for you."

I really didn't like it at all and certainly didn't want it. So I explained that I couldn't possibly accept such a gift from someone I hardly knew, "but thanks anyway." He merely shrugged, said it was no problem, and offered it to the waiter, who snapped it up with glee, proclaiming that it would fit just perfectly in his apartment! Had I missed something? Was this guy compulsively generous or was he just desperate to get rid of the lamp? (If it was the latter, I completely understood.)

I decided to go with the flow. After all, I had refused the gift, so he had a right do whatever he wanted with it. But that was not all Ted had up his sleeve. He promised that the next time we met, we would go to "Hot Tub Heaven," as he had a membership there! Unfortunately we couldn't go tonight because he had a very early meeting the next day. He asked for my home number, and when I wouldn't give it to him, he asked for my cell phone number. I told him I didn't have one, at which he dived into the briefcase and brought out a phone. "Here, have this. The number will come on when you turn the power on, okay?" Of course I refused the phone too, which seemed to be the last straw for generous Ted. He said I was behaving like a kid and should grow up. I agreed. I looked at my watch and saw that it was almost nine o'clock, time for all good kids to be safely at home. ❤

Luke, 31
Pen Salesman
SINGLE

When we had talked on the phone, Luke was so eager to know my shoe size that I assumed he had a foot fetish (or should that be "feetish"?). Anyway, I told him I was a five, my English size, forgetting that the American equivalent would be seven and a half.

As soon as we met, Luke handed me a bag and said, "These are for you." Inside was a pair of shiny red platform shoes with spike heels so high they'd make you tip forward as you walked. Not to put too fine a point on it, the only person who would be comfortable in those shoes is someone who spent a lot of time on her back. I'm sure it's what the most stylish hookers wear these days, but not this girl! Whatever they were, they were not my size. Luke was upset that they wouldn't fit me, and apologized.

I told him it wasn't a problem, but to him it was. He looked at his watch and said he would take me to a store and buy me another pair; if we hurried we could make it before the store closed. When I passed on his offer, he got angry. "I only want to buy you some shoes," he said. "I'm not going to take my dick out and rape you, for God's sake." That's quite correct, Luke. Not for God's sake, or anyone else's sake for that matter! I took to my size seven and a halfs and headed home . . . for *my* sake! ❤

Christopher, 49
Production Line Worker
SINGLE

Christopher asked me to meet him for lunch and named an Italian restaurant I had never heard of. His directions ended with "It's near Dunkin Donuts."

As I entered the shopping plaza he had mentioned, I saw him standing outside the Italian restaurant. In his hands he held a box from the doughnut store. I introduced myself and he did the same. Then he handed me the doughnut box, saying, "These are for you." I thanked him and was heading towards the restaurant when he said, "Since we have the doughnuts, we don't need to go to lunch, do we?" He suggested we could sit in his truck, eat the doughnuts (there were twelve), and he would buy us a drink—any drink I wanted, he offered magnanimously. According to Christopher, all the women he met from the personals liked to sit in his truck, eat doughnuts, and "bullshit"! I guessed that he couldn't afford to dine in the restaurant, and I was contemplating offering to pick up the tab for our lunch. I was about to suggest this when Christopher opened the box of doughnuts and took one out, coughed, spat on the sidewalk, and then popped the doughnut into his mouth. Suddenly I had lost my appetite.

What kind of women was this man meeting, that they found him appealing? Still, I guess it's an original approach. It just didn't work for me. ❤

Sammy, 32
Convenience Store Manager
MARRIED

Sammy wasn't able to spare much time away from his job, or his home, so he asked if I would go to his store for a soda. I wasn't keen on that, so he then asked if I would meet him at the subway. No again. Finally Sammy said that we could meet for a quick drink at a bar near his store, and we set a time. I was quite intrigued by now. What was he doing answering ads when he was married, and on top of it had no time to meet?

He turned up at the bar with a box full of groceries that included diapers and baby food. He handed me the box, explaining that he'd had to pretend he was doing a delivery. Hence the box of groceries. But guess what? He wanted *me* to pay for them! He figured that if he'd had to gather all the goods together so that we could meet, then I should have the decency to pay for them! Me pay? Not on your nellie!

The total, he calmly informed me, came to $28.63. When I told him that I wouldn't, he became quite flustered. What should he say about the delivery, or the non-delivery, he demanded. I asked whom he had to tell; after all, he was the manager, right? At that he picked up the box, threw it on the floor, and stormed out. As I left, the bartender was picking through the box like he'd won the supermarket sweepstakes. Well, Sammy, you made someone's day. ❤

Neil, 36
Realtor
MARRIED

I had a nice chat with Neil and was actually looking forward to meeting him after we arranged our lunch date. Imagine my surprise, then, when Neil turned up with his four-year-old daughter in tow. Not only was he a married man, he was also a daddy. And not only to this child; the older daughter was out shopping with his wife. Apparently, he couldn't risk bringing *her* along on our date, as she might tell on him. Another charmer!

Neil's daughter was very cute, but she was very clingy and didn't speak much. After about half an hour Neil excused himself to go to the men's room. When he had gone the child looked at me and asked if I would like to see her daddy's peepee. I told her that was a bit rude, but she looked indignant and said, "He *wants* you to touch it!" I began to get a serious sense that something was amiss here and longed to bolt, but I didn't feel I could abandon this poor kid.

When he came back, the little girl said, "I said it, Daddy, I did it!" while Neil acted all confused, as if he didn't know what she was talking about. She was bouncing all over the chairs, which I decided was my cue to make a getaway. Neil asked me to take her to the bathroom before I left, but she began to shriek and cry, so I just grabbed my purse and ran. Neil called after me, asking if he could come to my home later that week where "we could be more private," but I didn't bother to answer him. Had this man truly set his child up to ask me about her daddy's pee-pee? Neil, if you read this, you really are a first-class creep. ❤

Kent, 54
Lawyer
SINGLE

Kent was around five feet eight, a balding, mustachioed brunet who dressed very conservatively and had a very quiet demeanor.

We met at a bar, and Kent arrived with both chocolates and flowers for me. I protested that I couldn't accept his gifts, but relented when he asked that I please just keep the flowers at least.

Kent didn't want to waste any time, either his or mine. Over drinks he told me he would like to strip and dance for me; how did I feel about that? Did he want to strip and dance here and now in the bar, I wondered. "No, of course not," he said, that would be silly! He wanted to do it when we were intimate. When I told him that I doubted I'd find it erotic at all, he whined, "Oh Rochelle, aren't you sensual at all?" Maybe not, but I haven't noticed that many aging attorneys prancing around the room at Chippendales, either. I told him I was leaving, as we were definitely wasting each other's time. In the cab I realized I had left the flowers behind, but there was no way I was going back. Kent might have decided to commence the show. ❤

Jack, 36
Delivery Driver
SINGLE

Jack had a surprise for me too . . . his sister! They were both on their way to visit the sister's boyfriend, who was in prison. Jack explained that it was his only day off and he decided to kill two birds with one stone (a poor choice of phrase if ever there was one). His sister, Diane, seemed to be quite nice. She told me that her boyfriend was in prison for murdering his previous girlfriend, but he was "just so sweet" and she "just knew" that this man would never hurt *her*! He was a changed man, and after all, some women really do know how to push men's buttons, don't they. I wasn't sure if she was asking or telling me, but I tried to repress the shudder her words sent down my spine. And I thought *I'd* ended up with some losers!

Jack was apologetic, saying they had to be on their way pretty soon, but he was very happy that he had stopped by to meet with me and was glad to see that I was a "feminine woman." He said *feminine* as "fema-nine." I was just very glad that they couldn't stay long. Jack promised that he'd call me again so we could "do this again, darlin'." I shook hands with them both and headed off to my house. They, of course, were headed to the big house.

Rather them than me!

I couldn't help wondering, though, if like her brother, Diane met her mates through the personals. See chapter 8, Diane; these jailhouse Lotharios are a dime a dozen. ❤

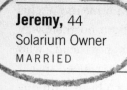

Jeremy, 44
Solarium Owner
MARRIED

The only weird thing about a conversation with Jeremy was that he wouldn't stop saying my name. Our conversation went along these lines:

HIM: "Rochelle, I'd really like to meet you, Rochelle."
ME: "Okay then."
HIM: "Rochelle, let's meet tomorrow, Rochelle."
ME: "Er, okay."
HIM: "Rochelle, I know a very good restaurant where we can get acquainted, Rochelle."
ME: "I said okay!"

Anyway, we did meet in the very nice restaurant and although his looks weren't much to write home about, he was very confident, and I was impressed in spite of myself. Not for long, however. After a couple of drinks, Jeremy put some ice into his mouth and crunched it loudly in a way he must have thought provocative. Then he asked me to turn around and look towards the bar. What did I think of the female in the blue suit? he asked. She looked dowdy, frumpy even, and I turned back to Jeremy and asked what was going on. Did he know her? Perhaps you'll be less surprised than I was to learn that the woman in the blue suit was Jeremy's wife.

He asked if she could join us, and I told him certainly she could. (Oh yes, I was the queen of cool!) If I had been on a real date, I would have been hysterical now, but I wasn't, so I decided to act as if this happened every day of my life. To cut to the chase, these two were looking for a threesome, and this is how they went about it. Glynis, the wife, asked if I liked the idea of being the "missing ingredient." And I couldn't help myself, I started to laugh, mainly because this couple reminded me of Sunday school teachers, not swingers looking for the filling for their sexual sandwich!

As I sat between the two of them, I felt decidedly uncomfortable. Glynis was smiling at me and complimenting me on my hair color, even going so far as to stroke it. Enough. Sorry, guys, you're too much for me. I'll just be "missing" if it's all the same to you. ❤

Jerry, 60
Nursing Home Proprietor
SINGLE

When I returned his voicemail message, I found out what Jerry did for a living in the course of his telling me about some builders he had working on his house. It seems he was none too pleased by their work, and I empathized with him just to be polite as he droned on about how they were taking weeks longer to finish than they had originally promised. "Oh, well, what do you do," I asked, striving for a philosophical tone that apparently went over Jerry's head because he came out with, "I own a nursing home. What do *you* do?" I might not have needed to ask if I had waited until our date.

We arranged to meet for lunch, and when I spotted Jerry I saw that seated next to him was a very elderly man. By elderly, I mean this man looked as if he could be a hundred and ten! Jerry introduced himself, and then gesturing towards the elderly man, said, "This is my father. He's very old and I never leave home without him. I hope you don't mind. He won't be any trouble; he can't hear and he can hardly see." Maybe he loved his dear old dad and was concerned about him, but even so. To bring him out on this particularly chilly day struck me as odd.

In fact Dad *was* no problem whatsoever. He sat slumped in his chair and slept most of the time. Jerry told me that he himself was "very athletic sometimes," whatever that meant. He didn't look athletic—in fact quite the opposite. When he asked if I had ever "had" an Italian-American man, I suggested the conversation was getting too personal, what with his aged father seated beside him. (I know he was hard of hearing, but still.) Apparently Dad's presence wasn't going to put a damper on Jerry's day. He went on at length about his sexual prowess. He could still "get it up" without a problem although he was sixty. He even told me that his father had only recently stopped having sex! (This little old man looked as though he couldn't raise a smile, let alone anything else, but who knows.) This was becoming a very unpleasant afternoon, and I wanted to cut it short. Jerry woke up his father and sort of slid him out of the restaurant. It was a funny sight, but I didn't laugh—it was too sad.

I never got the chance to ask Jerry why he had answered my ad, but I'd guess that he couldn't get out "alone" too much to meet women. Perhaps he should specify a woman with a very ancient mother of her own; things might work out then. ❤

Martin, 51
What I Do Is Private
SINGLE

Martin sounded very morose on the message he left me, and to be perfectly honest, it was tempting to erase him and go to caller number four. (No one would be the wiser, right?) But I stuck to the rules and called him back. He was still sad, but he wanted to get together and we arranged to meet on his day off. He promised that he'd tell me all his problems when we met! Martin sure knew how to keep a girl in suspense. I could hardly wait.

He had chosen a pizza place for our lunch date and was there when I arrived, sitting at a table, still in his raincoat. I hadn't really had a mental picture of him, but any picture I may have had wouldn't have prepared me for the reality of Martin.

He was a stout man and he wore the raincoat belted up tightly around his lumpy waist. It was almost as if he had stuffed small cushions or something under his coat. The buttons were straining, and I could see him beginning to perspire.

He shooed the waiter away and asked if I liked him. I responded noncommittally, but that was enough encouragement for Martin, who then told me "Shanie" had recently passed away. I had no idea who "Shanie" was, but I was sorry to hear it. He went on to describe how she had been hit by a car and it was he who had found her, which was all very traumatic for him. It had been almost two weeks since the accident and he was still upset. I felt sorry for him now, and agreed that to find someone you love dead in the street was too awful for words. When I said that, he opened a couple of buttons on the coat and reached inside to pull out the head of a dead cat! I ran out of the place and kept on running, nearly suffering the same fate as poor Shanie!

Martin left me two messages on the voicemail. The first was to tell me that he was sorry I had run away, as he had a couple of other animals under his coat that he would have liked me to see. The second was asking if I would feel more comfortable visiting with him at his home, where I could meet *all* of his animals!

Obviously, I didn't bother to call him back.

Of all the companions that came along with my dates, that was the worst. I would have rather had Glynis stroking my hair or Randy's obnoxious mother ignoring me. I never did find out what his job was, but on further reflection I decided I don't want to delve. It can stay "private" and probably should! ❤

nice guys
(it's not all bad out there)

If you have read this far, you must be feeling almost as jaded as I do. All those needy men and horny husbands can make a girl glad to be single. But it's not all bad out there. I met several really nice men, many of whom I would gladly have set up with a good friend or even seen again, had the circumstances been different. (Once I came clean about my greater goal, most wished me well and went on their way.) I won't bore you with the details of several dozen pleasant meals and lively conversations with interesting, interested, well-read, and well-mannered men; it's not that fascinating. As Tolstoy might have said, all happy dates are the same. But do take heart in the fact that I can state unequivocally that there are some decent guys who use the personal ads.

So why were they using the personals? A couple had recently moved into the area and didn't know many people. A few were divorced and had their kids most weekends, so had few opportunities for meeting women. Others just found it difficult to hook up with "the right woman" for various reasons.

Now before you take me to task for scaring off or otherwise mistreating the few good apples in this wormy barrel, you should know that only one became even a little upset when I explained my quest. But even he calmed down when I promised that I wouldn't reveal his full name and address. Mind you, he was exceptionally attractive and if I did name him, he would be inundated with calls. But he was embarrassed at having answered an ad, so I won't blow his cover. The rest all took it with good humor, and most insisted on paying for our date even though I made it clear it was my treat.

All of them had jobs, and two were quite high-profile. Quite a few said they had never answered an ad before, but a few others told me they had dated a little via the ads. They hadn't found the right woman yet, but they're still out there trying. So don't despair, there may still be a knight at the end of the tunnel. Read on. Don't skip these pages just because none of these guys are fully paid-up members of the cheating, lying, slave-worshipping association. Sometimes it's nice to be normal.

Aaron, 31
Golf Pro
SINGLE

I met Aaron in Miami. He said he was new to the area and was finding it difficult to meet women, as most of the people he met through business were men. Aaron was medium height, with dark hair and blue eyes. The only odd note was his jeans, which were too long; he had folded them up by several inches. His designer shirt didn't quite go with the redneck jeans. He explained he had just purchased his attire for our date—what could I say? Over pasta and salad and a couple of glasses of wine, Aaron said he had not had a girlfriend for three years and that's why he had answered my ad. In fact he had answered five ads in the last couple of weeks, but only I and one other had contacted him. He had not liked the other woman as she had chain-smoked throughout their date.

We chatted pleasantly about nothing in particular, and when Aaron asked why a woman like me would need to place an ad, it was time to tell him the truth. I explained about my mission and apologized for meeting him under false pretenses. Bless him; he was really interested (or good at pretending) in all the people I had met. He asked if I was going to include him in my book and seemed pleased when I told him I would if he'd like me to. He thought for a while and then said, "Yeah. I've got nothing to hide and maybe I'll get some publicity for my club." I didn't quite understand how going in my book would drum up business for him. But then again, women who want to meet a man could do worse than sign up for lessons with an attractive golf pro. In Europe, nine times out of ten, women who take skiing lessons end up letting Sven or whoever teach them something more than the snowplow!

I offered to pay for our dinner but Aaron wouldn't hear of it. He kissed me good-bye, and I promised to send him a copy of the finished book.

Oh, he asked me not to mention his jeans . . . so forget I mentioned them! ❤

Marvin, 39
Boat Charter Company Owner
SINGLE

This was a wonderful date, and not just because Marvin was good to look at or because he was extremely generous (although that's no bad thing). He was simply a fun guy.

When I called to arrange our date, Marvin suggested we meet up on one of his boats for the afternoon. That would have been excellent, but I didn't know him well enough, so I had to say no. When we did get together at a restaurant of my choice, he was the sweetest man you could wish to meet, and very funny. He didn't try to pressure me into anything odd, didn't reveal any strange quirks or deviant sexual fantasies. He seemed to be the man who had it all, and I had to ask why he was answering a personal ad. The simple answer was he wanted to meet new people and have some fun. No big deal, no ulterior motive. That was it! Based on my experience with him—and my experience with hundreds of losers—I tend to believe him. We had a nice afternoon and I thanked him for meeting me. He said he hoped I'd had fun and to call him if I wanted to do it again.

He was a definite candidate for the "nice guy" section, although on second thought, maybe he should go in the oddball chapter—it's truly a curiosity how such a man could be single! ❤

Mark "did" the weather for a local TV station. I wasn't sure that he'd have a lot to say, other than "It's hot again" (this was another Florida date), but apparently there was more to Gulf weather than sunshine.

It seemed that Mark's true forte was telling jokes, and while some of them were a little off-color, he was extremely funny. We met at a place on the bay where you can sit outside and watch the boats go by, where he was obviously a regular. Everybody there loved him.

Mark wore shorts and a T-shirt, and a baseball cap with the name of his station embroidered on the front. He was a little drunk when I got there, and more drunk when I left. The alcohol didn't impair his sense of humor, though, and he cracked jokes all evening long. (What do you call a lesbian dinosaur? Lickalotapuss!)

I never did find out what brought him to the personals—or come clean and tell him why I was really there. I tried telling him what I was up to, but after pouring so many Margaritas down his throat I'm not sure he really got it. But the laughs never stopped, and it was really good fun.

The next morning I watched him on TV, and there he was looking none the worse for wear. All in all, he'd been a fun guy and I'd had to tolerate a lot worse things than nonstop jokes.

Thanks for the date, Mark. ❤

Vincent, 33
Broker
SINGLE

A nice date and a very nice man! On the phone, Vincent had mentioned that his sister was coming into town; would I mind if she came along on our date? I thought it was a little strange, but what the heck. We decided on a time and place, and we had a little chat about nothing in particular. He sounded intelligent and upbeat, and I was quite looking forward to our date.

As it turned out, Vincent's sister didn't come with him. Her luggage had been lost and she wasn't very happy, so she decided to stay at Vincent's. Her loss, as we had a very pleasant time.

Vincent was very tall; he said he was six feet six and I believed him. His black hair was swept back and he wore a very smart suit. He asked why I had placed an ad, as he didn't see why I would have a problem meeting men. (Bless him!) I asked him the same question, and he admitted that he didn't really have a problem meeting women; he'd just answered an ad for a change.

Halfway through our meal, Vincent asked if I would like to go dancing afterwards, and I decided then to tell him the truth. He took it very well. In fact he claimed he thought it was a super idea for a book. As I knew he would, he asked about the other guys I had met and cringed when I related some of the weirder stories, saying, "I'm embarrassed to be a man!" Then he called his sister to check on her, and when he told her about me, I heard her laughing on the other end, so it seemed everything was all right.

I offered to foot the bill for the date in light of my revelation, but Vincent wouldn't hear of it. I promised that I would say only nice things about him, and it was easy to keep my promise. ❤

Steven, 30
Construction Worker
SINGLE

Tall, blond, tan, and muscular. That's how Steven described himself to me. Sound good? It was. Better yet, Steven was also a very nice man.

He had suggested we meet at a restaurant known for having fun with its patrons. I wasn't too sure what I was letting myself in for, but off I went.

I needn't have worried. The staff was hilarious and all their jibes were in good fun. Steven told me he answered ads quite often, and he consistently brought his dates to this place. It was relaxed, and even if his date was a drip, they really couldn't help but have a good time. Good thinking, Steven!

He also said that he wasn't looking for a relationship and didn't like to be tied down to one woman. He felt it was only fair to let me know where he was coming from. That was my cue to be just as fair in return. When I let him in on my project, he was hysterical and wanted to know what section he was going in. When I said he fit right in to the "nice guy" section, he pleaded with me not to make him come across as a "boring loser." That was an easy task because Steven really was an extremely good guy. ❤

Barry, 45
Picture Framer
SINGLE

Barry told me that he looked like Jack Nicholson, and when I met him, I was amazed at the resemblance. Sadly he sounded like another famous personality—Mickey Mouse! The voice and the look didn't go together at all.

Barry asked the usual questions as to why I placed an ad, and I didn't have the heart to dissemble. I fessed up, and I apologized for getting him there under false pretenses. After a few seconds of silence he asked, "What are you going to say about me?" I told him that I wouldn't include him if he were offended. To which he responded, "Hey, it's the best thing that's happened to me in years. Go for it."

We had a nice dinner, and a good chat. Barry insisted on paying the bill, lest I say that he was cheap!

So thanks for the date, Barry. You were one of the nice ones. ♥

Gregory, 42
Tattoo Artist
SINGLE

Here is a classic case of "Don't judge a book by its cover." In fact when Gregory entered the restaurant, quite a few people looked like they wanted to run for cover—me included! Gregory was very tall, liberally tattooed, and had a beard that would put ZZ Top to shame.

He ordered a soda (he told me he doesn't drink alcohol), and we chatted about England and ourselves. It wasn't long before he popped the question: Why I had placed an ad? Even though he looked a little intimidating, I went ahead and told him I was on my way to one thousand Americans—adding quickly that the evening was on me. He sat twisting his beard without speaking and then he smiled. Eventually he began to laugh.

Whew!

He ordered us more drinks, and told the waitress he was going to be famous. As our date was ending, Gregory invited me to Daytona for race week, so I guess there were no hard feelings. He roared off on his motorcycle, leaving me with a whole new attitude about the aging Hell's Angels I see riding around on their Harleys. ♥

Leo, 35
Pilot
SINGLE

Hey, ladies. A good-looking single pilot, and he's a nice guy too!

Leo said he had been answering ads for three years because he didn't want to date the women he worked with. He didn't have a very high opinion of flight attendants, though I could think of quite a few men who would disagree with him. Dating through the personals was exciting to him, and there was always the chance you might meet the love of your life, he said. I agreed.

This was clearly a good egg, so I decided to let him in on my goal. Far from being upset, Leo was adamant that he be included here. He spelled out his last name for me and asked only that I not mention the airline he flew for. He even asked if I needed pictures of him!

Leo has called ten times since we met, leaving nice messages and adding little bits of information about himself for "his" story. Here it is, Leo! ❤

Terry, 33
"Almost" a Realtor
SINGLE

Terry spoke really fast on the message he left. He wanted to meet up because he didn't get a chance to meet new women and also he was very busy. So I went along, wondering what to expect.

I was there on time and he arrived about ten minutes late, just as I was wondering if I had been stood up. He came charging in carrying three or four books, a calculator, some cards, and papers. What was it all about?

Terry was taking a crash course in real estate, eight to six for seven days. He ordered a beer and asked me to quiz him on the material, which I did. Consequently I now know that under Florida law the government can take private land for public use by "eminent domain." And Fannie Mae and Freddie Mac are not people on your mother's side that you don't like much; they are, in fact, types of mortgages. Terry justified this somewhat unusual date activity by pointing out that this information was useful, quoting that old favorite "You never know when you'll need it." I agreed . . . I don't know *when* I'll ever need it.

I certainly wished him well in his studies, but after three hours of HUD homes and quit-claim deeds, I had had enough. I bid Terry farewell and went home to my 3-bed, 2½-bath house with great location, location, location! Space in the yard for a pool and close to all good schools. The only thing missing from the sales spiel was "Mrs. Clean lives here," 'cos that's definitely not me! ♥

Donald, 33
Flea Market Trader
SINGLE

Donald had his stall in a market that attracted lots of tourists. On the weekends, especially during July and August, the place was packed with English holiday-makers, he reported. Donald's stock in trade was fake Mont Blanc pens. (He showed me a few, and they looked really authentic!) Donald was quite tall, with red hair and a medium build.

When we met for drinks, Donald said he needed one badly, that he'd had a rough day. I feared I was in for another night of shrink-on-the-cheap, but I needn't have worried. Donald was at pains to tell me that he wasn't "like all the others" who answer ads. And when I looked relieved (after all, I practically do *know* all the others), he asked how many men I had met through the personals. Since I could already tell that this date didn't promise any shocking revelations, I decided to let him in on my secret.

He took it really well. In fact, a little too well. He asked who was the best date, which was the worst, where was the best place I had gone to, and what I was going to say about him. I answered his questions as best I could and promised to forward his name to anyone who wanted to date him from reading my description. We said our good-byes, and Donald gave me two of his pens. Both wrote really nicely for a week, before they dried up. Ah well, it's the thought that counts, and I thought Donald was quite a decent guy. ❤

Gary, 39
Carpenter
SINGLE

I was assured that I would have a wonderful time if Gary and I met. He also admitted that he wasn't looking for a relationship, just someone to have dinner with occasionally, and asked if that was okay with me. Of course it was; right up my alley, in fact. We arranged to meet in an Irish bar that featured a comedy act.

Guess what? We really did have a wonderful time. He turned out to be a specialty chair designer, which was quite fascinating. The comedy act was hysterically funny—I have never laughed so much in one night. The place was packed solid, and everyone seemed to be having a great time.

When the comics took a break, Gary and I had a chance to talk again. I found out that he fancied himself a comedian, too, and he had done his routine on amateur night. He told me a couple of jokes that I didn't understand but I laughed anyway (not easy to do when something just isn't tickling your funny bone).

I wanted to tell him about my real reason for being there before I left, but he held his hand up as if to silence me and said, "I don't want to know. I don't care if you're married or if you're really a man. I had a great time tonight and I hope you did too." He wouldn't let me speak, just kissed me on the cheek and wished me the best. Oh well, I tried. Surely he didn't really think I was a man! You've just been watching too many Jerry Springer shows right, right, Gary? ❤

Neil, 38
Accountant
SINGLE

They say accountants are boring, but in this instance they would be wrong. I'm still not too sure who "they" are, but I know it's a worldwide organization, as no matter where you go, "they" always have a comment. Anyway Neil was tall, good-looking, well dressed, and funny too. He wasn't looking for a relationship, just some female company. He was originally from Pennsylvania and had only been in town for six months. I told him what I was doing, and he wanted to know all about the men I'd met and the places I'd been to. Then he was curious to know how he rated, and I told him without a doubt he was the nicest man I'd met— and it was true. Ladies, they are out there. If you have to date a few zeros before you meet the hero, men like Neil make the search worthwhile. ❤

Dave, 49
Barber
SINGLE

Dave didn't make a terrific first impression. He was too eager to tell me he owned his own shop, had several employees, and made a good living. His hair wasn't a compelling advertisement—he sported the Steven Seagal look with a big bald spot on top! And he didn't look as much like a barber as he did a hired gun (you can tell I've been in America too long). He completed the look with Versace sunglasses. (It had been a nice day, but it was eight o'clock in the evening now!)

But Dave turned out to be a lot of fun, so first impressions and all that can go out the window. He dished about all the famous people he "does," who is nice and who tips well. When I told him about my book, he wanted to know if I had met anyone famous. At the end of the evening he pronounced me a "helluva" girl and told me I must be careful, as there are lunatics running around out there.

Don't I know it, Dave. ❤

Bobby, 40
Store Clerk
SINGLE

Bobby and I had a nice date at a pizza place. The food was so delicious that I have since been back three times. (And who says I wasn't looking for a lasting relationship?) Bobby arrived still wearing his name tag from his work, so at least I knew he wasn't lying about his name.

I knew the store he worked for. In fact, he was the second date I'd had from that company. He hoped to soon be made a manager.

When I asked why he had chosen to answer my ad, he looked puzzled and said, "I thought you answered *my* ad." I assured him that he had definitely responded to my personal ad and he continued to look confused until I told him not to worry—we were here now and it didn't matter!

Bobby had recently moved into a new apartment and asked if I would like to visit with him when he had finished decorating. I said that would be nice, but I might be going back to London soon. He gave me his e-mail address and promised he'd mail me pictures when he had time (though I hadn't given him my address). I told him I had to get going, and when I paid the bill, he thanked me over and over again.

I'm sorry if I haven't done justice to Bobby. He was a nice man, just not my cup of tea! ❤

Grant, 38
Electrical Company Employee
SINGLE

Although Grant spent half our date on the phone, he was a nice enough man, just a very busy one. When he wasn't speaking on the phone, he was fiddling with it, twisting it all around and making it do little dances in time to the music. He apologized for the interruptions, but he had to be contactable at all times.

Grant had responded to my ad because he was too busy to meet women any other way. He said he found it hard to sustain a relationship when he did manage to find someone, for the same reason. So I told him about me and my goal of meeting a thousand men. He looked aghast, and even after I told him that I saw him sitting firmly in the "nice guy" section, he still wasn't happy. He asked what other sections there were, so he could decide if he should "slot" into a different category.

After he had heard all the other categories, though, he was happy to be a "nice guy."

Not long afterwards, we decided to call it a night. I offered to pay the bill, and he laughed and grabbed it from me. "I'm a nice guy, remember?" he said. I left the restaurant just as he took what must have been his fifty-sixth call of the evening.

He is here in the nice guy section, but only by the skin of his teeth! ❤

Todd, 40
Infrastructure Technician
SINGLE

Todd was such a sweetheart that our date was one of the few times I genuinely felt bad about luring a man to meet me with ulterior intent. When I spotted him at the Chinese restaurant we'd chosen, he was a sight for sore eyes. His description hadn't done him justice at all. At just under six feet tall, with sandy hair and green eyes, Todd was truly a looker! There's more. He was funny and intelligent (well, he'd have to be—look at his job title) and an interesting conversationalist.

We chatted about his job, mainly because I had no idea what an infrastructure technician did, and I found out that he had set up computer systems all over the country. As he traveled quite a bit, he hadn't found time to sustain a relationship, but now he was slowing down a little and hoping to meet someone.

Oh dear! I had to tell him there and then that I was here on a mission. Bless his heart, he smiled at me and said, "Good for you. Have you discovered that all men are bastards?" I told him that I'd known that long before I started my research, which he took in good humor.

In fact he was such a good sport about it all that I asked Todd if he would like to meet a girlfriend of mine. They have been out a couple of times, and whenever he's in town, they hook up. It's not a "love thang" yet but it's coming along nicely, thank you! ❤

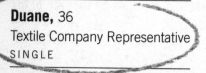

Duane, 36
Textile Company Representative
SINGLE

Duane was on vacation from a small town in Georgia, so this time I was the one to say "I love your accent," and I really did. Since he was from out of town, I recommended a restaurant. When he arrived, his first words were "Hey girl." Then he sat down and the fun began. He apparently specialized in "redneck" jokes, which were all new to me. I didn't even know what a "redneck" was, but judging from Duane's repertoire, they are the types who sell their car for gas money and whose goldfish drown! (Don't blame me, these came from Duane.) He had another couple of dates lined up, so he apologized that he wouldn't be able to meet up again that week. I told him that was quite okay with me, and we said our good-byes. I found Duane to be a nice guy, though I don't know what the rednecks would feel about him. ❤

Dexter, 35
Lawyer
SINGLE

A nice guy who's a lawyer? Can it be? Yes, it's true.

Dexter had a great personality. He was nice looking and he had a very sexy singing voice, which I know because he sang to me over dinner! It sounds corny, but I actually enjoyed it. He told me he had answered my ad on a dare. He and a colleague had been browsing through the paper, saw my ad, and they had both responded. Dexter was a bit smug that I had called him back and not his friend. He had no idea that he had been caller three, and his friend hadn't. So I had to tell him.

"Oh, man," he said. "I was jibing my friend that I had gotten a call back and he didn't, and it's only because I was number three?" I told him it was better than being a number two! He looked really mad for a while, but then he started to laugh.

I had to promise that I would describe him as a "sexy, black, woman magnet that I wanted in a way that I had never experienced before," which I happily agreed to. I bought him a glass of Champagne and we spent the next two hours very enjoyably. Dexter jokingly said that he should really draw up a contract and have me sign it to make me keep my promise! Thanks, Dexter, you gave new glamour to lawyers! ❤

George, 41
Auto Mechanic
SINGLE

When we spoke on the phone, George came across as quite shy. He said he had "never done anything like this before" and was a little nervous. He wanted me to choose the time and the place, and said he would fit in with whatever I came up with. I helped him along, and between us we managed to make a date for dinner.

When I first set eyes on George, I wanted to say "Aww," and I had to fight the impulse all through our date.

He was medium height with brown hair and a nervous smile that bordered on a twitch. He was biting his bottom lip and looking around the restaurant in despair. When I introduced myself, he said, "Oh, I was hoping you wouldn't turn up!" He immediately clarified that he hadn't meant it to come out like that. It's just that if I had stood him up, then he wouldn't have had to face me.

But guess what? Once reticent George had downed a drink or two, he wasn't quite so timid. In fact he became extremely verbal. I learned he had been married for twelve years when his wife asked him for a divorce. He hadn't particularly wanted to split up, but she was adamant, so they parted company. She got the house and he got the monthly payments. (Sounds fair to me.) After eight months his wife had a change of heart, and after a long talk they decided to try the marriage thing again. But before they did, his wife wanted him to get them a bigger house; in fact, she had seen one she just loved. So they got the bigger house and they moved in together.

Happy ever after?

No.

After four months, she told him it "just wasn't working."

She got the bigger house. He got the bigger bills. *Awww.*

Dear poor George, bless him and his cotton socks. How was I going to tell him about my ulterior motives after all that?

But when George asked about me, I decided that at least one woman should be upfront with him, so I came clean. He took it well and asked if he would be going in. I told him of course he would not, as I respected his privacy, and I said that I would also get the check for tonight's date.

He acted as though he were hurt at being left out and said that since everyone knew his wife had "done a number" on him, he wasn't particularly worried about having his story told.

So here is George, a nice man. A guy who makes you go *Awww!* ❤

David, 39
Record Producer
SINGLE

When David arrived at the restaurant for our date, he had a red rose for me, which was a nice gesture. Then he ordered Champagne and told me to order whatever I wanted. He was a tall man, casually but expensively dressed, and while we dined he told me he lived in Los Angeles but was here in town on business. He named some very well known recording artists that he had worked with. While he had had a couple of long-term relationships, he'd never been married.

David said he'd answered my ad for a bit of fun, but he did have a bit of an ulterior motive. (Well, he wasn't the only one, right?) David wanted to learn to speak English with an accent like mine. He wanted me to go to a studio with him and make some tapes so he could take them home and practice. He hastened to add that he would pay me. I wasn't sure if he really meant it or if this was the modern version of "Come up and see my etchings," so I said I'd think about it and call him. But as we parted company, I watched David walk over to a convertible Bentley gleaming in the sunshine. He waved as he drove off, oblivious to me calling out after him, "I'll do it! I'll do it! Come back," as he glided smoothly away. ❤

Geoff, 45
Cable Repairman
SINGLE

When I spoke to Geoff on the phone, he called me "Ma'am" and told me that he would love to meet with me, even if it was only for dinner. I wondered what he meant by "only for dinner." What else was he expecting from the menu? We decided on a day for our date, and then Geoff asked if nine-thirty was okay. That was really too late for me, and I asked if he could make it earlier, or even another day if he was busy. I wondered if he had an AA meeting or a shrink appointment.

Turns out, he couldn't make it any earlier as he "had" to watch *Hollywood Squares*. That wasn't over until eight o'clock, and then it would take him at least an hour to get into the city. He agreed he could make it by nine o'clock, and that was the best he could do. I was a little concerned that a middle-aged man would arrange his social life around a game show. Not that *Hollywood Squares* isn't a fun program, but still!

When the appointed evening rolled around, Geoff was on time and so was I. He was tall and nice looking, wearing beige pants and a black shirt. Black, very shiny boots completed the outfit. I thought maybe the *Hollywood Squares* thing was really an excuse for something else. But no, it seems he was a true aficionado.

I made the mistake of asking about that evening's episode. That set the tone for our date. He spoke about nothing else. He recited all the questions and I had to answer as best I could. He loved Whoopi Goldberg, but there were one or two guests that he wasn't keen on and the female contestant was apparently "spaced out." Bruce Vilanch was great (as always, apparently). It was quite bizarre. He then brought out a *Hollywood Squares* quiz book and asked if we could play while we had our dinner. I had nothing to lose, and at least he wasn't rude to me, or to anyone else, which is always a plus, so I went along. He ate with one hand and held the book in the other, all the while asking or answering questions.

When the waiter asked if we would like dessert, I said I was full, but Geoff wanted some cheesecake. While he ate that, I asked more questions from the book. Then he was finished and so was our date. He shook my hand, thanked me for a wonderful time, and he asked if we could do it again next week. Or maybe I could go to his home and watch TV. He said he got cable for free, so he had a lot of channels. I thanked him and said I would see about that.

Before he left, he took the napkin from the table and shined the already gleaming black boots. That done, he wished me "Goodnight, ma'am" and he was gone. ❤

what I learned
(this is a short chapter!)

If anyone is expecting me to be full of wisdom and all "clued up" on the how, why, and what of men's minds, I'm afraid they'll be disappointed. Even with all this dating behind me, it's still a hit-or-miss business finding someone to spend some time—or even share a meal—with. But I have gleaned a few crumbs that may be worth passing along.

Many people have been curious about the regional variations among the men I encountered, and whether American men are much different from those I dated back home. In a word, no. Cheating, married men were as abundant in all the states I visited as they were in the U.K., though I have to say they were more prevalent in New York, as were the submissive men! Men from the Midwest lived up to their reputation as more conventional, less worldly than their coastal cousins. (In fact, I only stayed there for three weeks before moving on, as all the guys I met were so "normal" I couldn't get much of a story out of those dates.)

My experiences in the Deep South were erratic; initially, I found the men there pretty nice, then in one week I met three of the strangest men in America! So you take your chances in the hinterlands. And Florida stands alone as having the most unpredictable dating pool, perhaps because there were so many tourists and transients, or maybe because there is so much new money (and other substances) floating around down there.

East or west, several universal truths did begin to emerge after a couple hundred dates. It seemed that the older the man, the younger the women he was hoping to date! And no matter what a man looked like—pot belly, receding hairline, and all— he held himself in amazingly high esteem and had the high standards to go along with it. I was called too skinny, too old, too unappealing by men I wouldn't have looked at twice on the ATM line.

Secondly, your chances of winding up with a married man are appallingly high. I still don't know why so many men feel the need to cheat. One particular middle-aged, overweight fool told me, "I don't want to sleep with other women. I just need to know that I *can*"! I honestly believe these men do not understand the pain and heartache that their infidelity can cause. (Just like they don't understand why we hate the thought of them going to strip joints and giving their money to "Sacha," who in turn gives that money to "Peter," her boyfriend, to put him through school.) My sad conclusion is that most men would cheat if they thought they could get away with it, so if you don't want to waste your time on someone who's already taken, make that clear from the start.

Those caveats aside, I do think the personals can be a valid and fun way to meet people and maybe, if you're lucky, find a true soul mate. Even after all these dates, I still love going out to dinner with someone new—and not only because I can't cook! However, you should certainly be far more discriminating in who you choose to get together with than I was. Were I to undertake this journey again in earnest I would do the following:

• Be specific about the type of man I was hoping to meet. I don't expect every guy who answers my ad to be a wealthy professional with flowing auburn hair and chiseled abs, but I would ask if he had hair and teeth. Exact height and weight, please, especially if he asks the same of me!

• I would be sure to ask if he had a penchant for anything remotely kinky. If he said yes, then I would run in the other direction.

• I would word my ad more carefully. "Fun times" was a cheeky phrase that I knew would intrigue a lot of men; most thought it meant sex, though it meant something else to me and to my girlfriends. However, avoiding innuendo of any kind is definitely advisable if you're not eager to fend off Mr. "I know what you need, baby."

Most of all, just have fun. If you go into the process with low expectations (and I mean really low) you won't be disappointed. And who knows, you may hit the jackpot. Remember that the old adage "appearances can be deceiving" is true (for better and for worse, I'm afraid). Don't let down your guard in a way that could compromise your safety, but give the guy a chance. I never ceased to marvel at how different most men were from the initial impressions I formed of them, and their true colors and personal charms often emerged only after a bit of candid give and take. So be aware, but be open. In almost every case, if you lean forward and ask someone, "Tell me about you," the words will start to flow. Every man's (and woman's for that matter) favorite subject is himself, so if you're truly interested and willing to listen, you should never be at a loss for conversation. After that, it's up to you. ❤